# The Crafter's Guide
## to
## Glue

### Techniques & Projects

## Pattie Donham

Sterling Publishing Co., Inc.
New York

## Prolific Impressions Production Staff:

Editor in Chief: Mickey Baskett
Copy Editor: Ellen Glass
Graphics: Dianne Miller, Karen Turpin
Styling: Lenos Key
Photography: Jerry Mucklow, Steve Wilcox
Administration: Jim Baskett

Library of Congress Cataloging-in-Publication Data

Donham, Pattie.
  The crafter's guide to glue : techniques & projects / Pattie Donham.
    p. cm.
  Includes index.
  ISBN-13: 978-1-4027-3501-1
  ISBN-10: 1-4027-3501-4
  1. Handicraft. 2. Gluing. I. Title.

TT157.D633 2007
745.5--dc22

10 9 8 7 6 5 4 3 2 1

2007007543

Published by Sterling Publishing Co., Inc.
387 Park Avenue South, New York, N.Y. 10016
©2007 by Prolific Impressions, Inc.
Produced by Prolific Impressions, Inc.
160 South Candler Street, Decatur, GA 30030
Distributed in Canada by Sterling Publishing
c/o Canadian Manda Group, 165 Dufferin Street
Toronto, Ontario, Canada M6K 3H6
Distributed in Great Britain by Chrysalis Books Group PLC,
The Chrysalis Building, Bramley Road, London W10 6SP, England
Distributed in Australia by Capricorn Link (Australia) Pty. Ltd.
P.O. Box 704, Windsor, NSW 2756 Australia

Printed in China
All rights reserved

ISBN: 13: 978-1-4027-3501-1
ISBN: 10: 1-4027-3501-4

For information about custom editions, special sales, premium and corporate purchases, please contact Sterling Special Sales Department at 800-805-5489 or specialsales@sterlingpub.com.

## Acknowledgements

I thank these manufacturers for their generous contributions of quality products and support in the creation of the projects in this book:

Coats & Clark, Greenville, SC, www.coatsandclark.com, *Pattie Wack Pompom & Tassel Tools, yarns & fibers*

Duncan Enterprises, Fresno, CA, www.duncancrafts.com, *Aleene's glues*

Beacon Adhesives, Mt. Vernon, NY, www.beaconcreates.com, *a complete line of glue for every surface including 3-in-1 Tacky Glue, Fabri-Tac, Gem-Tac, and more*

Glue Dots International, New Berlin, WI, www.gluedots.com, *Memory Book Glue Dots*

Xyron, Inc., Scottsdale, AZ, www.xyron.com, *Create-a-Sticker Dispenser and other laminating machines*

3M/Scotch, St. Paul, MN, www.3m.com

Hammerhead, Ontario, Canada, www.hammerhead.com

Tape Systems Inc., Mt. Vernon, NY, www.tapesys.com, *Adhesive Sheets*

Krylon, Cleveland, OH, www.krylon.com, *All-Purpose Spray Adhesive and other spray adhesives*

Provo Craft, Spanish Fork, UT, www.provocraft.com, *Pattie Wack/Coluzzle Templates, Coluzzle Scoring & Cutting Tools, brads, eyelets, and scrapbooking papers*

EK Success, Clifton, NJ, www.eksuccess.com, *scrapbook papers, stickers, and paper cutting system*

K1C2, Ventura, CA, www.k1c2.com, *Adornaments Fibers & Yarns*

Crafts Etc!, Oklahoma City, OK, www.craftsetc.com, *brads, grommets and brackets*

Delta Technical Coatings, Whittier, CA, www.deltacrafts.com, *Sobo Glue*

Artistic Wire, Ltd., Elmhurst, IL, www.artisticwire.com, *Art Wire*

Janome, Mahwah, NJ, www.janome.com, *Memory Craft 6500 Sewing Machine*

Jacquard Products, Healdsburg, CA, www.jacquardproducts.com, *Pearl Ex Powdered Pigments*

Art Institute Glitter, Inc., Cottonwood, AZ, www.artglitter.com, *3-D Embossit Adhesive, and leafing adhesive*

Crafter's Pick/API, Inc., Albany, CA, www.crafterspick.com, *The Ultimate Fabric Glue*

Wrights, West Warren, MA, www.wrights.com, *ribbon and trims*

# About the Author

## Pattie Donham

With her "down home" spirit, professional background, and experience, Pattie Donham has been crafting everyday things into extraordinary art for more than 20 years as a designer, television host, product consultant, and author in the world of crafts. Known by her friends and fans as "PattieWack," she is as wacky, disarming, and kind in person as she seems on camera. Her talents range from paper crafts, stamping, sewing, yarn/fiber crafts, quilting, mosaics, candles, floral design, scrapbooking, and jewelry making to kids' crafts.

Pattie's diversity is unmatched, and includes experience as an author/designer for more than 18 booklets and dozens of magazines. Pattie was a host on "Aleene's Creative Living" television program, and has appeared on numerous national TV shows, including "The DIY Jewelry Making Show," "Home Matters," "Our Home," "QVC Home Shopping," "Home & Family," Home Shopping Network, and currently as host of "Let's Craft!" video series for the Creative Home Arts Club.

Pattie Donham has developed several new box templates and paper craft tools used for creating unique designs such as the high-heeled shoe and teapot seen in the following pages. Her craft studio is filled with little paper boxes in every size and shape you can imagine. Other apparent obsessions include tassels and pompoms. "My greatest inventions so far are the PattieWack™ tassel and pompom tools," says Pattie.

Southern California is where Pattie resides, but Oklahoma is her home state where she travels frequently to be close to her family, which includes two daughters and four grandchildren. She stays busy with her husband, Scott Wilkinson, and their video production company, Craft TV Studios, which is a leading provider of instructional videos for the crafts industry.

As founder of PattieWack Designs, her extensive experience developing and designing craft products includes creative alliances with Coats & Clark, EK Success, K1C2, LLC and Provo Craft. In her spare time Pattie enjoys writing the PattieWack Newsletter, adding to her blog, and updating her website at www.PattieWack.com.

# Preface

I love to craft! Having worked as a craft designer and product developer for the last 20 years, I feel very lucky to have a "job" that feeds my craft habit. Someone recently told me that I must have been born with a bottle of glue in one hand and a sewing machine in the other, and I think they were right. I was raised in a minister's home. My mom and I were always planning Bible School projects, sewing our own clothes, or creating handmade crafts for the next charity fund-raiser.

I was thrilled when I was asked to write a book about crafting with glue. One of my crafting mottos is, "If you can't glue it, I won't do it!" Glue is pretty much a necessity for nearly every craft project I encounter. I have no idea how many glue guns and how many bottles, tubes, and containers of glue are in my possession.

About a dozen years ago, this obsession with glue led me and my crafting accomplice, Darsee, to pour handfuls of beach sand into a big bowl of white glue. Like two mad scientists, we giggled ourselves silly as we created our first mosaic masterpiece with our "secret" grout recipe.

Another glue incident happened one day when Darsee and I were scouting for just the right props for yet another segment for "Aleene's Creative Living" television show. We spotted some beautiful stained glass sun catchers, and at the same time turned to each other with identical twinkles in our eyes, saying, "We could make that with napkins!" We could hardly contain ourselves as we sped back to our studio to glue napkins onto glass for our first reverse collage experience.

I've come a long way since Bible School projects and the reverse collage incident. At the same time, glue and adhesive products have evolved over the last few years. There are so many adhesives that some stores have an entire aisle dedicated to this very important crafting ingredient. Sometimes I feel that I have earned a degree in "glueology." As I researched glues and adhesives for this book, I was amazed to discover more and more ways to create fabulous handmade crafts and stunning art with the help of a little glue.

You're invited to explore the applications, techniques, uses, tips, and projects in this book. If you enjoy crafts, be my guest in the quest to unlock the secrets of glue.

*Pattie*

# Contents

# CHAPTER I

# Crafter's Guide to Glue

Most of us have a few favorite glues we reach for every time a sticky situation arises for a craft project. Sometimes, however, we look at the pieces we plan to stick together and scratch our heads about which glue to use. Instead of scratching our heads, let's take a look at some of the types of glues and their uses for crafting. Keep in mind that the following information is to be used as a guide, so always check the label on the glue to make sure it meets your requirements.

# White Craft Glue

The number one glue most crafters reach for is the all-purpose white craft glue. In fact, I always have at least two bottles on hand because I certainly don't want to run out of glue in the middle of the night, in the middle of a crafting marathon. I use white glue in my grout and bread dough clay recipes, as you will read later on.

The thicker white craft glues usually have the word "tacky" as part of their names. It is usually less messy and items will stick together faster. White glue is usually in a squeeze bottle, but other packaging variations include tubs and spritzers.

**Characteristics:** The glues in this category are usually polyvinyl acetates, which is a synthetic polymer. These glues are water-based, non-toxic, non-acidic, odorless, nonflammable, and require only soap and water for cleanup. They dry clear and flexible. They work best on porous surfaces and shouldn't be used to hold heavy objects together, or items that will be washed. Their biggest strengths are that they are non-toxic, are easy to clean up, and can be used on a variety of surfaces, making them ideal for children's crafts.

**Uses:** Use white craft glue on porous and semi-porous surfaces like paper, wood, chenille, leather, yarn, and some non-washable fabrics like felt. Because it does not have a strong bond, it should be used only on lightweight objects.

# Hot Glue

I will never forget my first glue gun. You would have thought I had discovered the hottest new invention since the wheel. Everything in the house became embellished. Everything, that is, except the family pet – although, if I remember correctly, the kitty collar was immediately covered with rhinestones and gems.

There are many new choices of glue guns since my early glue gun days. Now we can choose cool melt, hot melt, or a combination of both with a dual heater, an automatic shut-off, an on/off light, protected nozzle, and a battery pack. All that's left is a glue gun holster to match my outfit.

There are also many choices for glue rods, also called glue sticks, to use in the guns. The rods are designed for various sizes of glue guns. Be sure to check the packaging to make sure it works for the surfaces you will be gluing. The standard color for glue sticks is clear, but there are colored glue sticks to match project needs and for embellishing. Glue sticks can also be heated in a glue pot, which melts the glue into a pool for brush application or for dipping. This approach can be especially useful for floral arranging.

To dissolve a bond, hot glue can either be picked off or reheated with the tip of the glue gun or a hot hair dryer. Please be careful not to touch the nozzle or the hot glue. I like to keep a bowl of ice water handy in case my finger accidentally gets in the way.

**Characteristics:** Hot melt glues are thermoplastics. The glue rods are placed into a glue gun that heats the glue. The glues are applied hot and allowed to cool and harden. The low temperature glue guns heat the glue to a temperature of about 250 degrees F (120 degrees C). This low temperature glue is best for delicate work and children's crafts. The higher temperature guns heat the glue to about 380 degrees F (195 degrees C). They dry quickly – faster than white glues or fabric glues. Hot glue may loosen when exposed to extreme hot or cold temperatures, so I do not recommend using it for outdoor projects. The bond will last through only a few washings.

**Uses:** Use hot glue to bond a wide range of porous surfaces such as silk flowers, fabrics, chipboard, and wood. Do not use on foam or other soft plastic that could melt.

# Epoxy

Sometimes epoxy is just the thing for a project that needs a super strong bond. My glass teacup birdfeeder can perch on top of a copper pole because of this glue.

**Characteristics:** Usually epoxy glues come in two parts. When you mix the two parts together, the resulting glue forms a tough and durable synthetic resin that can withstand relatively harsh conditions. One-part epoxy glue is also available; "one-part" means it is pre-mixed and does not have to be mixed by the user. Epoxy glue dries very clear, but can form air bubbles. It may take 30 minutes to an hour for the surfaces to bond. It should be allowed 24 hours for a proper bond.

**Uses:** Epoxy is best used for wood, metal, masonry, glass, ceramics, rubber, vinyl, leather, and fiberglass. Epoxies are NOT recommended for paper, foam, fabric, or children's crafts.

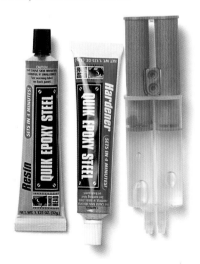

# Decoupage Glue

The traditional decoupage technique requires hours of sanding and layers upon layers of lacquer varnish over very intricate papers with fine detail. I have a great respect for decoupage artists. As a crafter, I use the word "decoupage" loosely to describe gluing paper to a project.

**Characteristics:** There are some wonderful modern decoupage glues available for crafters that bond, coat, and seal the paper to the project in one easy step. These one-step decoupage glues are available in matte and gloss finishes. Cleanup is easy with soap and water and yet the finish is water-resistant when dry. Many of these glues look like white glues and most are non-toxic and water-based.

**Uses:** Decoupage glue works well for gluing cards, gift wrap, stamps, posters, decoupage papers, magazines, color copies, and photographs to papier mache, terra cotta, wood, canvas, glass, plaster, and foam. It is also good for children's crafts.

# Liquid Laminate

For reverse decoupage or decoupage under glass, you may also use laminate glue, which bonds, coats, and seals in one easy step. It is perfect for laminating fabrics, paper, napkins, color photocopies, lace, trims, and prints onto glass and plastic, as well as wood, metal, plaster, and terra cotta. Reverse decoupage on glass is one of my favorite crafts. I have found that it is best to test the paper to see if the ink runs before I glue it to my decoupage project.

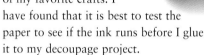

# Foam Glue

The number of craft foam cutouts that are available is unbelievable. Everything from foam doorknob hangers to foam photo frames are cut out and ready to craft. Foam glue makes this type of craft project easy because it's fast grabbing and ultra tacky. It grabs instantly, yet allows time for repositioning.

**Uses:** This craft glue is specially formulated to adhere colorful foam craft sheets to each other, including Styrofoam® brand and foam rubber. Foam glue is also ideal for bonding a wide variety of embellishments to the foam.

# All Purpose, Super Strength Adhesive

These adhesive gels are another glue type that is a must-have for the crafter. This glue creates a strong, instant, permanent, and water-resistant bond on many surfaces.

**Characteristics:** Industrial-strength adhesive delivers a high-performance bond. These glues are not water soluble and set up very slowly. They usually contain toxic substances which make them not a good choice for children's crafts. Some of these quick-gripping glues are specially formulated for outdoor use. Check the label to see if it will withstand heat and cold, is water-resistant, and contains a UV inhibitor. Indoor/outdoor adhesive gels are recommended for pottery, terra cotta, cement, resin, ceramics, rigid PVC, and wood.

**Uses:** The gel-like consistency is ideal for a wide variety of surfaces. Use for gluing wood, plastic, fiberglass, metal, jewelry, ceramics, rubber, glass, leather, and hard plastic.

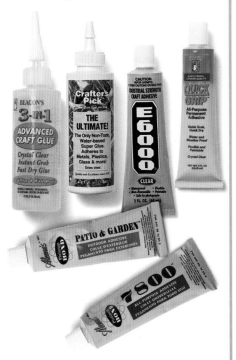

# Foiling Glue

You can create dazzling designs with the look of liquid metal with foiling glue. After applying glue and letting it dry, the next step is to press the dull side of a craft foil sheet into the glue, then pull the sheet away. The metallic foil remains on the glue.

**Characteristics:** This dimensional adhesive comes in a pointed-tipped applicator bottle, which lets you "draw on" your design. It goes on milky, then turns clear, but remains tacky when dry.

**Uses:** This technique works well on the edges of glass and china, on paper crafts, plastic, wood, home decor and non-washable fabrics. I like to use foiling glue for making broken china jewelry. The dimensional quality covers the sharp edges and is forgiving around jagged edges.

# Metal Leafing Glue

Leafing glue is used in conjunction with metal leafing sheets. The glue is applied using a brush to cover an entire surface, such as a picture frame. The glue dries clear and remains tacky when dry. Gold and silver leafing can then be adhered to the glue, and burnished with a soft cloth. It is best to brush sealer over the foil or leafing to protect your project from tarnishing.

# Jewel Glues

When you want to embellish an evening dress or a fancy project with rhinestones, crystals, sequins, gems, pearls, or beads, you need dependable glue. Embellishing glues are perfect for slick to porous surface applications.

**Characteristics:** Choose either clear gel permanent bond glue, or white permanent bond glue. Some are flexible and made specifically for fabric. Others work on non-porous surfaces such as plastic, glass, and metal.

**Uses:** They are also great for bonding lace, fabrics, trims, and decorative wire to glass, ceramics, patent leather, wood, vinyl, and leather.

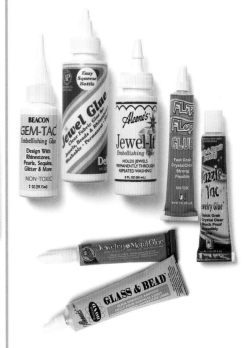

# Glass & Metal Glue

**Characteristics:** These adhesives grab fast, are water- and weatherproof, and are UV resistant. They dry clear, flexible, and strong.

**Uses:** These glues are great for bonding ceramic, glass, plastic, and mirror to glass, wood, and terra cotta. Use this type of glue for doing mosaics. With the growing popularity of mosaic crafts, you can find glue that is expressly packaged for this technique.

# Paper Glues & Tapes

The phenomenon of scrapbooking and paper crafts has caused a storm of new glues and adhesives. Every time I go to the craft store, there are more sticks, bottles, tubs, and tubes of glue. When you are shopping for glues meant for paper, they fall into two specific categories. There are archival glues that are acid free and safe for photos, and there are standard glues.

Scrapbooking adhesives should be archival, acid-free and lignin-free. If you don't use glues with these qualities, your photos are in danger of becoming damaged after a period of time. Check the labels and be sure the glues are specially formulated for use in memory albums.

Following are some of the types of paper crafting glues and adhesives you will find:

**Glue Sticks:** These are non-toxic, washable, and acid-free. They dry fast, won't warp or ripple the paper, and apply smoothly. Some glue sticks are colorful adhesive when you swipe them across a page, then they dry clear. There are also photo glue sticks available that are made especially for photos so your beautiful treasures will last through the years.

**Liquid Paper Glues:** These glues are formulated with less water, and are quick to dry so the paper doesn't swell and wrinkle. They are available in squeeze applicators with a variety of tip options. Some adhesives dry clear, while others dry white.

**Vellum Glue:** Vellum paper can be tricky when it comes to gluing. Vellum can be seen through, so if you do not use the proper adhesive you will be able to see it through the paper. Look for an adhesive made just for use with vellum. You will be able to use this specialty paper with ease and your project will look beautiful.

**Scrapbooking Tape:** These are specially formatted for use with scrapbooking – acid and lignin-free. They won't discolor over time or harm photos.

# Kids' Glue

Doing crafts with kids is the ultimate learning and play experience. There are many types of glue that are non-toxic and super thick for easy projects. Check the labels and choose adhesives that do multiple tasks for paper, wood, felt, leather, shells, beads, sand, fabric, cork, glitter, or cardboard.

If you choose glue that is specifically for foam crafts, be sure the glue is safe for children, and it is non-toxic. There are foam glues that are water-based, non-toxic and washable.

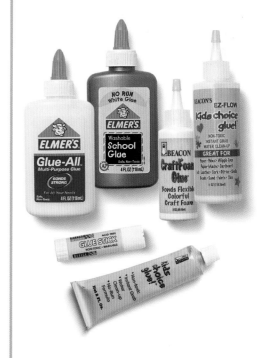

# Spray Adhesives

Spray adhesive comes in aerosol cans, and will not bleed through, stain, or wrinkle most materials. This glue is very handy for a quick and permanent bond. It adheres in seconds, yet has an extra long tack range that allows you to lift and reposition materials for some time after spraying. You can depend on long-term bonding of lightweight materials such as fabric, paper, cardboard, foams, felt, acetate, foil, and plastic.

# Silicone Glues

**Characteristics:** Silicone based glues can be used as a sealer as well as a glue. They are great for indoor and outdoor use because they are water-resistant, good in high temperatures, and won't break down in cold weather. When dry, they are flexible and will retain their dimension. The drawback is that they are very thick, so a smooth bond is not possible. The biggest problem is that these glues are very toxic and it is best not to use them around children.
**Uses:** They are excellent for gluing glass, metal, and some plastics and rubbers. Testing may be necessary. Many crafters use this type of glue for gluing marbles and jewels to glass, mirror, metal, and ceramics. They are available in clear and a variety of colors.

# Fabric Glue

There are many types of fabric glues available that help you make a perfect appliqué or prevent the fraying of threads, or that will baste fabric together in order to sew a perfect seam. There are also fabric glues that will permanently bond a hem in a pair of jeans. Here are some examples:

**Permanent gel** is clear, works quickly and dries clear. It can be thinned with a small amount of acetone. You cannot dry clean a garment that has this glue application, but it may be washed. (Pictured: Beacon Fabric Tac, Aleene's OK to Wash-It, Leathercraft Cement)

**Permanent white fabric glue** can be used to bond fabric permanently, such as when making hems. You can also use it to glue trims to garments. This glue dries clear, and many dry flexible for stretchable fabrics.

**Temporary glues** are meant to hold until the item is washed. Some of these are labeled as basting glues. They come in squeeze bottles and as spray adhesives. They eliminate the need for pinning or basting while giving a strong, temporary bond to fabrics. I like to use basting spray to hold several layers of fabric together while sewing, such as when making quilting blocks. These temporary adhesives are also great for stenciling, embroidery, and appliqué.

*Fabric Glue, continued*

**Liquid fusible glue** fuses trims to fabric. It is applied and allowed to dry for 15 minutes, then ironed for a permanent bond. It is washable and dry-cleanable.

**Napkin applique glue** seals paper napkins onto garments and home decor fabrics. It is washable and dries clear.

**Fray preventive glue** stops fabric from fraying, and it dries clear, soft, and flexible. It's easy to apply and can handle repeated washings. I don't recommend it for ribbons, but it works great on seams, trims, cording, and braids.

**Fabric stiffener** is available in bottled form or as a spray when you want to stiffen a fabric, doily, or ribbon. You can repeat applications for desired stiffness, or wash it out for cleaning and reshaping.

**Fusible Web:** These paper-backed fusible webs are sold by the yard in pre-cut sheets, or in narrow rolls. You can find them in fabric shops. They are available in many different bond strengths; be sure to read the label to select the right one for your project. These are terrific for no-sew appliqués, interfacings, and hems.

# Double Sided Adhesives

Adhesives that are dispensed on a paper backing are very popular for scrapbooking and for a variety of crafting projects. These glues are available in many forms such as runners, sheets, dots, lines, squares, strips, tapes, foam backed, and through laminating systems.

**Laminating Machines:** Adhesive laminating systems are machines that are used to apply instant adhesive on the back of a piece of paper. They are great for creating your own stickers. They can also be used on parchment and vellum. Over the years adhesive runners for scrapbookers and crafters have become more advanced, offering a wide range of cartridge sizes that provide a path of glue from 1/4" to 12" wide. The cartridges are contained in pens, palm sized runners, and cartridge containers that have a crank that you turn. Some of the containers allow you to simply drop a cutout or small item into the opening on top, and then pull the paper from the bottom where the glue is attached to the item, ready to stick onto your project.

**Double-sided adhesive sheets, shapes, and tapes** are available in a variety of handy forms. Some come on sheets with a waxy paper backing and have a cover sheet. These types can be solid sheets or in shapes such as dots, squares, hearts, or stars. Other double-sided adhesives come on rolls, in pens, and in cartridge type applicators. I like to use the sheets and shapes for beading on hard surfaces and the tapes for holding heavy cardstock together when making boxes or dimensional paper crafts.

**Adhesive dots, squares, strips, and lines** are dispensed on a roll or on perforated sheets. They are quick to use, non-messy, and have an instant strong bond. Some of the dots of glue are thin, for a very smooth bond, and others are thicker to allow the items to stand out from the surface for added dimension. The glue is extremely sticky, so your embellishment is attached the instant you press it down. They can be used on a variety of surfaces to permanently bond buttons, jewels, charms, fabric, trims, and paper to plastic, metal, wood, foam, fabric, and paper.

**Foam tape and shapes** are great for mounting and layering items. They are acid free and are a favorite of paper crafters.

# Contact Adhesives

When you need a dry adhesive with a very strong bond, this is the answer. Contact adhesives are great for attaching leather and fabrics to surfaces such as wood, metal, and glass. To use this type of glue, both surfaces are coated, then allowed to dry until tacky. The surfaces are then pressed together. The glues are petroleum-based, containing toxic substances such as toluene or acetone.

# Hints & Tips:

### Glue or adhesive?
Technically speaking, glues are natural and adhesives are synthetic, but for ease, we will use both words interchangeably. Some modern synthetic adhesives are extremely strong, and are becoming increasingly important in modern construction and industry. The first glues were gums and other plant resins. Archaeologists have found 6000-year-old ceramic vessels that had broken and been repaired using plant resin.

### Read the label.
Glue is an adhesive substance used to bind or fasten items together, and there are different types of craft glue to suit the content and weight of the materials used across a broad range of crafts. Remember to read the label before you apply glue. You might be surprised to find out that both surfaces should be glued and then pressed together, or maybe you shouldn't apply any pressure at all. The labels will also tell you in what environmental condition the glue works best, how much time it takes to dry, toxicity, how to remove it, and other pertinent information you need to know.

### Prepare the surface.
Before you get gluing, prepare the surfaces of your project. Clean both surfaces thoroughly. Any dirt or oil may prevent proper bonding. You'll want to wipe metals, glass, and other nonporous surfaces with a degreasing agent, such as alcohol. If you're gluing wood, strip it free of any paint, wax, and varnish.

### Use glue sheets.
Work on waxed paper or freezer paper so your project won't stick to the surface. This paper can also be used to place over the glued area so you can press the surface to assure a good bond.

# CHAPTER 2

# Fabric & Leather Projects

Introduce new accessories into your home to update your decor immediately and even change the way your old pieces relate to each other. Fabrics and leather are great for adding color and texture, and these projects come together quickly with fabric glues, spray adhesives, or hot glue.

## Glues to Use

Fabric glue
Leather cement
Jewel glue
Permanent spray adhesive
Hot glue
Basting spray adhesive
Fusible web

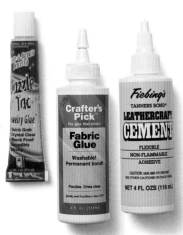

# Savoir Faire Shoe Bag

Instructions on next page

## SUPPLIES

**Glues:**

Jewel glue

Fusible web

**Surface:**

Handmade or purchased shoe bag

**Fabrics:**

Pink striped fabric

Dark pink fabric

**Embellishments & Trims:**

Pink acrylic gems, approximately 30 – ranging in sizes from 3mm to 6mm

Pink ribbon 2 yds. 1/4" wide (if making your own bag)

Pink pompoms, purchased or handmade with fibers of your choice *(See "How to Make a Pompom" in the "Live a Little Pompom Pillow" project, Chapter 2.)*

Pink ball fringe, enough to fit around bag

**Tools:**

Scissors

Iron & ironing surface

# Savoir Faire Shoe Bag

The cancan girls painted by Toulouse-Lautrec would have been happy to store their Parisian high heels in this sassy shoe bag, embellished with pompoms and beaded appliqué.

## INSTRUCTIONS

1. If you are making your own bag, sew in the ball fringe when you are attaching the front and back pieces together. If you have purchased a pre-made bag and want to add ball fringe, simply whip stitch it around the edge of bag.

2. Enlarge or reduce shoe pattern to size desired to fit onto front of bag. Trace pattern pieces for shoe onto paper side of fusible web. Cut out, leaving a 1/2" border all around.

3. Lay cutout fusible web pieces on back of pink fabric and pink striped fabric, with paper side facing up. Iron web to fabric, following manufacturer's instructions on package.

4. Cut out fabric, following patterns.

5. Peel off backing paper. Iron both pieces of fabric to the bag, placing the pieces of the shoe snugly together.

6. Glue gems to the appliqued shoe with jewel glue.

7. Make two pompoms and sew them to the end of the bag drawstrings. ❏

# Patterns

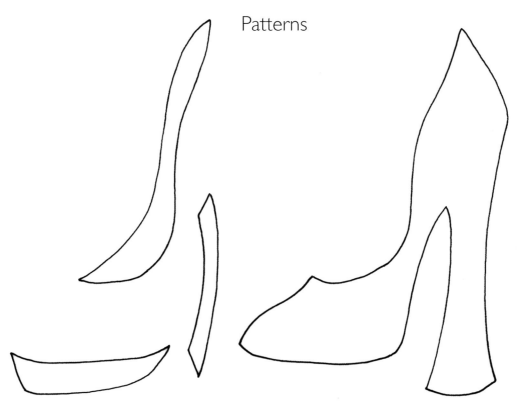

Cut from dark pink fabric.

Cut from pink stripe fabric.

# Eclectic Reflections Frame

Embellished with leaf charms made from bread dough clay, silhouettes of leaves cut from a rusty screen door, and colorful beads, this leather-framed mirror will reflect the welcome warmth of your home with each passing glance.

## SUPPLIES

**Glues:**
Leather cement
Hot glue or super-strength adhesive
White craft glue (for making bread dough leaves)

**Surface:**
Wood framed mirror, size of your choice

**Leather:**
Kidskin leather, 3" larger than frame all around

**Embellishments & Trims:**
Straight pins with glass heads
Assorted glass beads
4 eye pins, 2"
Jump rings

**Paint:**
Acrylic paints (for tinting bread dough clay)

**Other Supplies:**
Old screen door remnants or wire screening (sold in craft stores)
White bread, 1 slice for making bread dough
Plastic bags
Disposable bowl
Rub-on wax metallic finish or metallic mica powder

**Tools:**

| | |
|---|---|
| Chalk | Craft knife |
| Craft stick | Toothpicks |
| Wire cutters | Scissors |
| Hammer | Needle nose pliers |

## INSTRUCTIONS

**Frame:**
1. Remove mirror from frame.
2. Place leather face down on work surface. Place frame face down in center of leather. Use chalk to draw around inside opening and mark from corner to corner with an X. Draw around outside edges of frame. Set frame aside.
3. Cut the X from corner to corner in center of leather with a craft knife.
4. Apply leather cement to front of frame. Place frame face down on leather, lining up with chalk markings. Turn face up and smooth out leather on front of frame.
5. Apply leather cement to sides and inside opening of frame. Wrap leather around each side of frame, folding at corners.
6. Apply leather cement to back of frame. Wrap leather and smooth it into place along edges and opening.

**Leaf Charms:**
1. Prepare bread dough clay recipe. (See recipe in Faux Porcelain Roses project, Chapter 12)
2. Shape the leaves. While clay is soft, pierce a toothpick through top of leaf to create a hole for hanging. Let leaves dry thoroughly.
3. Rub with wax metallic finish or metallic mica powder.
4. Cut leaf silhouettes from the screening.

**Trim:**
1. Thread a bead onto a glass head straight pin. With wire cutters, snip off end of pin, making it 3/4" long. Gently hammer the beaded pin 1/2" from edge of the center opening on front of frame. Repeat all around frame opening.
2. Thread the eye pins with beads, forming the ends into a loop. Attach the loop to the screening silhouettes and dough leaves with jump rings to create four beaded leaf charms.
3. Thread each leaf charm onto a glass head pin. With wire cutters, snip off the end of the pin, making it 3/4" long. Gently hammer one pin in each corner of the frame.
4. Use hot glue or super-strength adhesive to glue the mirror back inside the center opening of the frame. ❏

# Heirloom Leather Scrapbook

Soft and supple kidskin leather invites you to touch, open, and peek inside this heirloom scrapbook embellished with feathers, antique buttons, and animal print. Imagine displaying keepsakes from a safari, or photos of days gone by, on the pages of this striking book.

## SUPPLIES

**Glues:**

Leather cement

Double-sided adhesive tape

**Surface:**

Scrapbook or 3-ring binder

**Fabric & Leather:**

2 kidskin leather rectangles, 2" larger than open binder on all sides

1 scrap piece kidskin leather with natural edge

Animal print plush fabric

2" wide strip of snakeskin texture black leather, 2" longer than binder

**Embellishments & Trims:**

3 feathers, longer than height of binder

Assorted vintage-style buttons

Assorted beads

Silver or pewter charms

**Tools:**

Colored chalk

Scissors

Sewing machine

## INSTRUCTIONS

1. Lay open binder on one of the kidskin rectangles. With chalk, mark 1-1/4" from edges of binder on all four sides. Cut along marks. This will be the outer cover.
2. Cut a second kidskin rectangle the same size. Fold in half to find center. Cut 1" away from fold, which will make room for inside spine of binder. This will be the lining. Set aside.
3. Glue snakeskin textured strip vertically onto front, attaching it approximately 3" from left edge of front cover. Glue with leather cement.
4. Referring to photo for size and placement, glue animal print fabric and leather edge remnant to right side of front cover with leather cement. Let dry.
5. Lay lining pieces on cover, right sides facing. There will be a gap in the middle for the spine of the binder.
6. Lay the binder on top, centering on spine, and mark leather 1/4" from binder edge on all four sides. Set the binder aside.
7. Sew a straight stitch on the marked line, on all four sides to attach the lining to the cover. Trim the seam.
8. Turn cover right side out.
9. Turn under raw edges at top and bottom of cover where the spine will be placed. Hold in place with double-sided tape.
10. Fold finished cover backward in the middle. Fold binder backward and gently slip the binder into the pockets of the leather cover. Fold binder back to normal position, easing corners into place.
11. Adhere vertical feathers with double-sided tape, overlapping them on each side of the black snakeskin strip. Trim ends of feathers even with top and bottom of binder.
12. Adhere diagonal feather in place with double-sided tape.
13. Adhere buttons with leather cement.
14. Cut strips of leather from leftover scraps. Thread beads on strips and tie charms to ends of strips. Attach to cover with leather cement. ❏

# Live a Little Pillow

Live it up with pink flamingos and pompoms that take your mind to fun times and faraway places. Giant pompoms add an unexpected touch to this whimsical pillow.

## SUPPLIES

**Glue:**
Fabric glue

**Surface:**
Fabric covered pillow

**Embellishments & Trims:**
Variegated yarn to complement pillow print

**Tools:**
Scissors

Pompom tool – or cut your own from cardboard

# INSTRUCTIONS

1. Make four pompoms, using the 4" tier of the pompom tool or a 4"-wide piece of cardboard. *(See instructions in box.)*

2. Glue a finished pompom to each corner of the pillow. ❏

## How to Make a Pompom

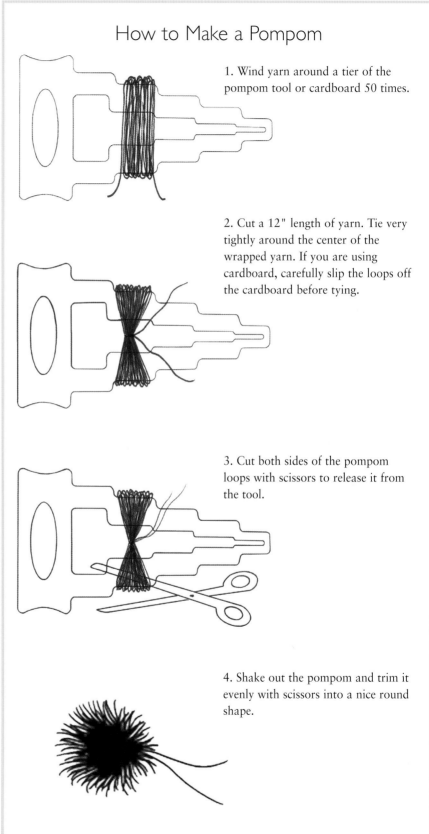

1. Wind yarn around a tier of the pompom tool or cardboard 50 times.

2. Cut a 12" length of yarn. Tie very tightly around the center of the wrapped yarn. If you are using cardboard, carefully slip the loops off the cardboard before tying.

3. Cut both sides of the pompom loops with scissors to release it from the tool.

4. Shake out the pompom and trim it evenly with scissors into a nice round shape.

## SUPPLIES

**Glues:**

Basting spray adhesive

Permanent spray adhesive

Hot glue

**Surface:**

3-section wooden room divider, black

**Fabrics:**

7 fabric pieces, 3/4 yard each

**Embellishments & Trims:**

Assorted upholstery trims

Gimp, enough to frame all 6 panels

Assorted buttons

*Optional:* Tassels, purchased or handmade with fibers of your choice *(See "How to Make a Tassel" in the "Secrets Scrapbook Page" project, Chapter 3.)*

**Paint:**

Black paint, if needed for room divider

**Other Supplies:**

Paper

Batting

**Tools:**

Scissors

# Bold & Beautiful Room Divider

Make a bold and beautiful statement in any corner with this crazy quilt room divider, covered with rich jacquards, raw silk, tapestry, and colorful upholstery trims.

## INSTRUCTIONS

1. Paint the wooden room divider, if necessary. Let dry.
2. Cut a paper template the exact size of one of the room divider panels.
3. Using the template as a pattern, cut batting for each of the six panels.
4. Arrange fabric pieces on paper template to resemble a crazy quilt design, cutting at angles to fit, making certain fabric edges meet evenly.
5. Spray one of the batting panels with basting adhesive. Place the cut fabric arrangement on the batting, pressing and smoothing to fit perfectly.
6. Hot glue assorted trims where fabric pieces meet, overlapping ends.
7. Spray back of completed panel with permanent adhesive. Adhere to one of the room divider panels.
8. Hot glue gimp trim around edge of panel, covering raw edges of fabrics and securing the fabric panel to the room divider. Turn under the end of the gimp and hot glue a button on top to finish.
9. Repeat steps to cover each panel.
10. Add button and tassel accents if desired. ❑

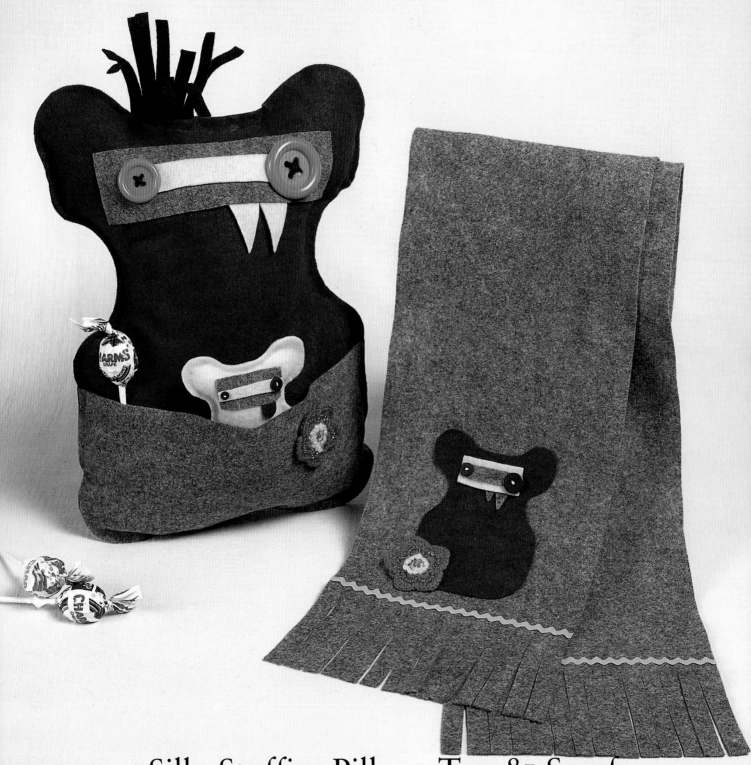

# Silly Stuffies Pillow, Toy & Scarf

"Lovable, huggable, and silly" describes these snaggle-toothed monsters. Make one
to wear around your neck, one to snuggle, and one to tuck inside a pocket.

## SUPPLIES

**Glue:**

Fabric glue

**Fabrics:**

1/3 yard burgundy felt

1/3 yard gray felt

1 square pink felt

1 square black felt

**Embellishments & Trims:**

1 large pink button, 3/4"

1 medium pink button, 1/2"

2 small black buttons, 1/4"

2 extra small black buttons, 1/8"

2 crochet rosettes

Pink rick rack trim

Black yarn

Pink yarn

**Other Supplies:**

Pillow batting

**Tools:**

Scissors

Clothespins

Needle

## INSTRUCTIONS

**Scarf:**

1. Cut out scarf from gray felt, measuring 8" x 60" (the width of the material). Cut 1/2" wide fringe on each end, 5" deep.
2. Glue rick rack along top of fringe on each end.
3. Cut out burgundy monster appliqué according to the pattern. Glue to one end of scarf. Using photo as a guide for face, cut out pink and gray strips and triangles, and glue to the top of the appliqué.
4. For eyes, sew one small and one extra small button onto the face with pink yarn.
5. Glue crochet rosette to bottom left corner of the appliqué.

**Stuffies:**

1. Cut out bodies, faces, and pocket for the stuffies, according to the pattern.
2. Glue face to burgundy body. Glue pocket onto body at sides and bottom. Hold together with clothespins until glue is set.
3. For eyes, sew one large pink button and one medium pink button to face of burgundy stuffie with black yarn. Cut fringe from black felt and glue

to underside of head. Hold with clothespins until glue is set.
4. Glue burgundy body front to burgundy body back on all sides, leaving an opening at the bottom to stuff. Hold with clothespins until completely dry.
5. Stuff body with batting. Glue body closed. Glue crochet rosette to pocket.
6. Assemble small stuffie in the same manner, without hair, pocket, and rosette. Sew on black button eyes with pink yarn.
7. Place the small stuffie inside the pocket of the large stuffie. ❏

## Patterns

Enlarge @145% for actual size.

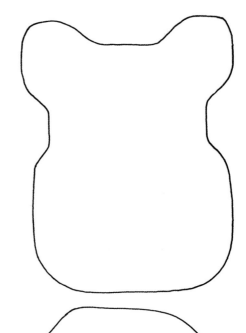

# Patterns for Silly Stuffies
Actual Size

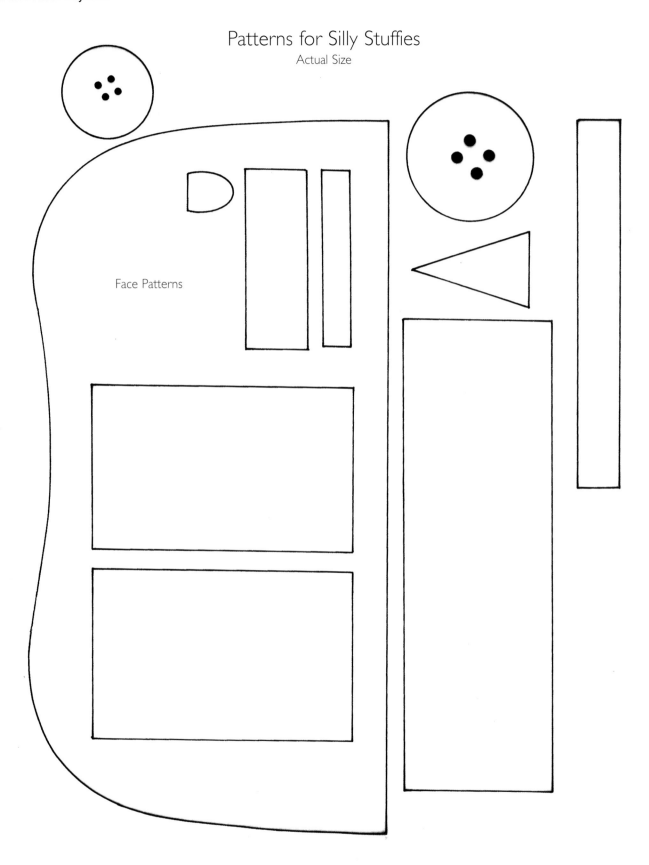

Face Patterns

## SUPPLIES

**Glue:**
Fabric glue

**Surfaces:**
Pillows, sizes to fit tank tops
Tank tops

**Embellishments & Trims:**
Iron-on appliqué of your choice
Sequin trim
Ribbon bows

**Tools:**
Scissors
Iron & ironing surface

## INSTRUCTIONS

1. Slip pillow into tank top. Trim excess length from bottom of tank top. Remove pillow.
2. Iron appliqué to tank top, following directions on package, or glue bows to straps and sequin trim to neckline. Let dry.
3. Turn tank top inside out. Glue bottom closed. Let dry. Turn tank top right side out.
4. Put pillow into tank top with bottom seams matching, and straps over top of pillow.
5. Remove tank top from pillow for laundering by hand. ❑

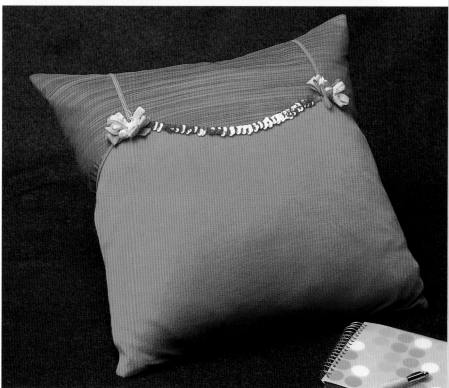

# Top That! Pillows

Tank tops turned into pillows are too cute! Pick a pillow that fits into your favorite top, adorn it with appliqués and bows, and toss it right onto the bed.

## PattieWack Pointer:
Another fun idea is to cover pillows with t-shirts from events in which your kids have participated. Simply slip the shirt over a bed pillow and glue the bottom closed, to create a memory pillow for their room!

# CHAPTER 3

# Paper Crafts

If you're like most of us, your first experience with glue also involved paper and scissors. All three of these have come a long way since we were in kindergarten. Scissors now cut jazzy decorative edges and adhesives are keeping pace with the demand for faster, cleaner, easier, and more secure bonds. Thanks to scrapbooking enthusiasts, it is easy to find an almost infinite variety of paper colors, patterns, and textures. Gorgeous gift wraps, metallic papers, and handmade papers with natural fibers stack up alongside brown paper bags as materials for crafting into everything from greeting cards to 3-D paper sculptures. Glue, paper, and scissors-they were fun then, but they're even more fun now!

## Glues to Use

Paper glue
Permanent spray adhesive
Laminating machine or adhesive runner
Adhesive dots
Double-sided adhesive tape
Vellum adhesive tape

## SUPPLIES

**Glues:**

Laminating machine, adhesive runner

Adhesive dots

Scrapbooking tape

**Papers:**

Antique script scrapbook paper,
  12" x 12"

Red roses scrapbook paper, 8" x 12"

Cardstock, black

Cardstock, beige

**Embellishments & Trims:**

Rub-on alphabet

8 gold eyelets and eyelet setter

Black and red fibers

**Tools:**

Scissors

Craft knife

Cutting mat

Tassel tool – or cut your own from
  cardboard

*Optional,* Frame Templates

# The Red Dress Scrapbook Page

An elegant scrapbook page is a beautiful way to show off a glamorous photo of Mom in her red dress, surrounded by roses.

## INSTRUCTIONS

1. Put rose print paper through the laminating machine adhesive runner (or spray back with spray adhesive). Adhere to script paper, offset to right of center.

2. Cut a strip of black cardstock 3" x 12". Adhere across top of page as shown in photo, using the laminating machine adhesive runner or spray adhesive.

3. Cut frames from black cardstock using purchased frame templates, or measure and cut with a craft knife. Cut large frame to 6-1/4" x 5" for outside dimensions, making it 3/4" wide. Cut small frame 2-3/4" x 5" for outside dimensions. Round the corners of the frame if desired.

4. Cut a strip 3/4" x 5", and three 2" squares with rounded corners from beige cardstock.

5. Apply rub-on letters to beige squares and strip.

6. Set eyelets in beige squares, using the photo as a guide.

7. Make three 3" tassels, leaving hanger ties 8" long. *(See "How to Make a Tassel" in the "Secrets Scrapbook Page" project, Chapter 3.)* Thread hanger ties through eyelets of beige squares. Adhere beige squares to black cardstock with adhesive dots. Wrap hanger ties to back of page and secure with scrapbooking tape.

8. Adhere beige strip to smaller black frame with adhesive tape runner. Set eyelets as shown in the photo.

9. Add Mom's photo and frames to page with adhesive tape runner. ❏

# "I Do"
# Journal & Bookmark

This unique and original wedding journal is entirely handmade, using foam core board for the covers. Add grommets and bind with a lovely tassel to create a cherished keepsake for the bride as she captures every memory from the proposal, engagement, shopping trips, parties, and romantic private moments.

## SUPPLIES

**Glues:**
Paper glue
Spray adhesive
Jewel glue
1/4" double-sided adhesive tape
Vellum adhesive tape
*Optional:* Laminating machine

**Surface:**
1/4" foam core board, 14" square, 2 pieces

## Papers:

Assorted coordinating cardstock and scrapbook papers

Vellum papers

## Embellishments & Trims:

Square alphabet brads, to spell groom's name

Round alphabet brads, to spell bride's name

Round decorative brads

Small round brads

Label holder

1/4" embroidered ribbon

1/4" pink organdy ribbon, approx. 2 yards

Braid trim

Large pearl monogram (or you can make your own by gluing strung pearls into a letter shape)

Art wire

Assorted yarns & fibers

Small string of pearls

10 eyelets and eyelet setter

3 grommets and grommet setter

## Additional Supplies:

Binder ring

"I just love you" rubber stamp

Background script rubber stamp

Block design rubber stamps

Embossing ink

Clear embossing powder

## Tools:

Scissors

Decorative edge scissors, scallop cut

Craft knife

Metal edge ruler

Pencil

Permanent marker

Hole punch

Heat gun

Tassel tool – or cut your own from cardboard

Pompom tool – or cut your own from cardboard

Embroidery needle

# INSTRUCTIONS

### Journal:

1. Cut two 12" diameter circles from foam core board for front and back covers.
2. Adhere scrapbook paper with spray adhesive to both sides of back cover.
3. Adhere scrapbook paper with spray adhesive to only one side of front cover. This will be the inside of the front cover. Set aside.
4. Cut a sheet of scrapbook paper to fit top left area of cover, using the photo as a guide.
5. Cut a sheet of coordinating scrapbook paper to fit bottom left area of cover, using the photo as a guide. Cut vellum paper the same size and adhere to paper with vellum tape.
6. Lay the two pieces of embellished papers together, and mark placement for eyelets, using the photo as a guide. Insert eyelets into both papers. Lay papers side by side. Beginning at left, lace organdy ribbon through eyelets, ending on right edge, to join the embellished papers.
7. Turn the joined pieces over and spray with adhesive. Adhere to front cover. Set aside to dry.
8. Cut a sheet of solid paper to fit top right area of cover, using the photo as a guide. Adhere to cover with spray adhesive or laminating machine adhesive runner.
9. Cut a coordinating paper to fit bottom right area of cover, using the photo as a guide. Cut vellum paper the same size and adhere to paper with vellum tape. Attach a border of decorative round brads along bottom, curved edge. Attach to cover with double-sided adhesive tape, along the curved edge only, to form a pocket.
10. Tear a 12" x 2" strip of solid paper. Adhere to cover as shown in the photo, covering edges of other sections.

### Add Trims to Cover:

1. Attach pearl monogram to paper at top left of cover with jewel glue. If you don't have a pre-made monogram, glue pearls into the shape of your monogram.
2. At bottom left quadrant of cover, glue embroidered ribbon 1" from top straight edge of the paper. Glue square alphabet

brads along ribbon to spell groom's name. Attach a label holder with small brads under name, and insert a paper label with the year written with a marker. Add small brads along bottom, curved edge of paper.
3. Stamp the top right quadrant of cover with background script stamp and emboss.
4. On the vertical torn paper strip, stamp with block design stamps and emboss. Glue round alphabet brads down center of strip to spell bride's name.

### Finish Journal:

1. Attach braid trim around edges of both front and back covers with double-sided adhesive tape.
2. Punch holes and set grommets in covers for the ring binder, using the grommet setter.
3. Cut several pages of scrapbook paper into 12" diameter circles. Punch holes to align with holes in covers. Bind covers and pages together with the ring binder.
4. Create a six-inch tassel with assorted yarns and fibers. Bind with a string of pearls. Tie to ring binder. *(See "How to Make a Tassel" in the "Secrets Scrapbook Page" project, Chapter 3.)*

### Bookmark:

1. Cut tag shape for bookmark from coordinating card stock.
2. Stamp and emboss "I just love you" on solid color scrapbook paper. Cut out oval shape with scallop edge scissors. Glue to hold in place, then whip stitch to bookmark using embroidery needle and fibers.
3. With embroidery needle and fibers, use a running stitch to create a border about 1/4" in from the edge all around the bookmark.
4. Punch hole and set grommet in bookmark.
5. Make a pompom using yarns and decorative fibers. Tie to grommet with the fibers. *(See "How to Make a Pompom" in the "Live a Little Pompom Pillow" project, Chapter 2.)*
6. Tuck bookmark tag in pocket on cover. The bride can use it to mark her place in the latest bride magazine while shopping for the perfect dress. ❏

# Altered Art Books

An *altered book* is a book that has been changed by an artist to represent something different from its original subject. I select a book and add to it, embellish it, and give it a new meaning. It can represent a thought, a fetish or interest, poetry, a relationship, or a journey. An altered book can celebrate an occasion such as a birthday or a birth, a wedding or anniversary, graduation, retirement, holidays such as Christmas, or even a family pet. The altered book is a form of art without boundaries or rules, inspired by the maker's personal experience and creativity.

*Open the Door* to creativity with this altered book, where an open window holds wooden game pieces that spell out the word "ART," and you are urged to compose music, dream, and grab a key to unlock the door to your own originality. Old jewelry, rubber stamps, charms, and even a hot wax kiss are used to embellish and inspire.

## Get started:

### Select a Book
Pick a book that is battered, used, and intended for disposal. Your library probably has books they will sell by the pound or by the inch, or give away to anyone who will take them. You may also find abandoned books at thrift stores. An old hardbound book with a textured, richly colored cover is a piece of art in itself. I love to find a book with sketches or notes written in it by someone in its past. Choose a book that "speaks to you" and your creativity will immediately be inspired to alter it into a new story, written by you!

### Gather Treasures
I find it easier to work with a theme. Gather rubber stamps, decorative papers, magazine clippings, and anything else that carries out the theme. You can represent a year with old dominos or dice. You can write words with game tiles. Charms, keys, old jewelry, ribbons, rub-on transfers, feathers, pressed flowers and leaves, locks of hair, beads, puzzle pieces, envelopes, tassels, beads and wire, fiber and yarns – whatever goes with your theme can be used.

### A Blank Canvas
Get out your acrylic paints and paint right over the cover of the book. Glue items onto the cover, poke holes, and tie on strings and beads. The cover will give the viewer a sneak peek at what awaits inside. Next, imagine the pages as blank canvas. You can glue, wire, or screw pages together; cut out windows, add drawers and peek-a-boo pages; or even add pages that can be unfolded to reveal more images. I like to glue sheer tissue over a page, paint or rubber stamp images, then add a collage of objects to give texture and interest.

### No Rules
Let your imagination go! Look through your treasures for whatever grabs your interest and sparks an idea. Find a focal point such as a photo, a sentimental brooch, a set of old keys, etc. Do you want the book to lie flat or display on an easel, be a keepsake box, hang on the wall, be a personal journal, or is it going to be a gift? Use spray adhesive to glue the pages together, and sprinkle glitter on the pages.

**Glue Away!**

Lay out the elements on your book until you achieve the look you desire. Cut windows and niches, then glue and attach the pieces together. As I always say, "Have fun with it!" ❑

*What I Have, Is What I Want* and you will want to write in this altered journal every day. A pop-up filled with motivational messages is glued to the front cover to welcome you inside. A tassel closure and golden inscriptions encourage you to take a little time to ponder your experiences and record them in your very own personal journal.

# You're Invited Invitation

This dance recital invitation pops with excitement! It is easy to
create with a template and stickers that relate to the event.

## SUPPLIES

**Glues:**

Adhesive runner

Vellum adhesive

Adhesive dots

**Papers:**

White cardstock

Peach cardstock

Patterned vellum

**Embellishments & Trims:**

Organza ribbon with peach borders, 2" wide

Pink fibers

Alphabet stickers

4 daisy stickers

Ballet theme stickers

2 daisy bouquet stickers

2 peach eyelets & eyelet setter

**Tools:**

Scissors

Craft knife

Bone folder or scoring tool

Cutting mat

Metal edge ruler

Pop-up template

Permanent marker

## INSTRUCTIONS

1. For card cover, cut white cardstock to a size that will accommodate the pop-up insert. Score and fold in half.
2. Cut peach cardstock 1/2" smaller all around than front of card. Adhere to center of card front with adhesive runner.
3. Cut vellum paper 1/4" smaller all around than card front. Adhere over the peach paper with vellum adhesive.
4. Cut peach cardstock 1" smaller all around than card front. Adhere alphabet stickers to spell "You Are" in the center. Adhere cardstock to vellum with adhesive runner.
5. Cut organza ribbon 2" longer than width of card front. Wrap ribbon from side to side, adhering to inside cover with adhesive dots. Add fibers in the same manner.
6. Place a daisy sticker on each corner of peach "You Are" panel.
7. Place the pop-up template over a piece of peach cardstock. Cut and score according to template directions.
8. Adhere pop-up inside card with adhesive runner.
9. Adhere alphabet stickers to spell "Invited" on upper part of pop-up insert.
10. Adhere ballet stickers and daisy bouquet stickers to pop-up sections.
11. Attach eyelets to card with eyelet setter.
12. Write invitation information inside card with permanent marker.
13. Braid fibers together to form two cords. Tie through the eyelets. ❏

*Template pattern on page 40*

# You're Invited
# Template Pattern

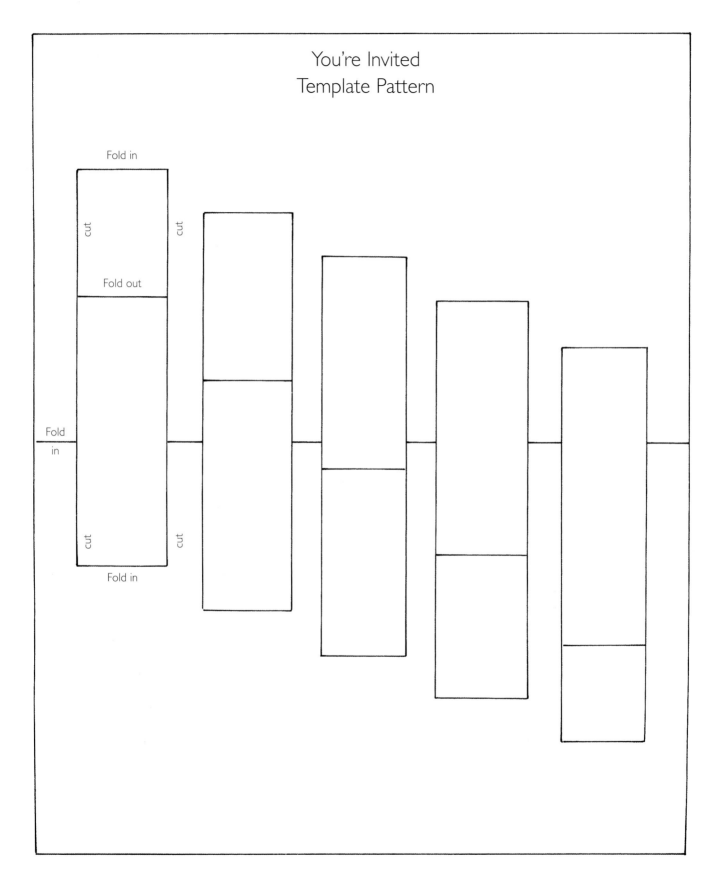

# Second Hand Style Hanky Dolls

Make fabulous skirts for these paper dolls with vintage hankies.
They are just as much fun to make as they are to give away.

## SUPPLIES

**Glues:**
Spray adhesive
Double-sided adhesive tape

**Surfaces:**
Heavy white cardstock
Paper dolls *(color photocopies work well)*

**Embellishments & Trims:**
Vintage handkerchiefs

**Tools:**
Scissors

## INSTRUCTIONS

*Use purchased paper dolls or color photocopies, or print out paper doll images from sources on the internet. Remember: copyrighted materials may not be sold, but copied only for your personal use.*

1. Adhere paper doll copies to cardstock with spray adhesive. Cut out dolls.
2. Fold hanky in half diagonally, from corner to corner.
3. Fold the folded edge over about 1-1/2".
4. Slip doll behind hanky, with folded edge as a sash at the waist.
5. Turn doll face down. Fold hanky corners down to the doll's feet, then fold back to form a train for the skirt.
6. Hold in place with double-sided tape between folds of skirt. ❏

# Let-r Rip! Gift Boxes

Rip out gorgeous pages from your most glamorous
magazines to make these pretty gift boxes!

## Template Pattern

Enlarge or reduce for package size of your choice.

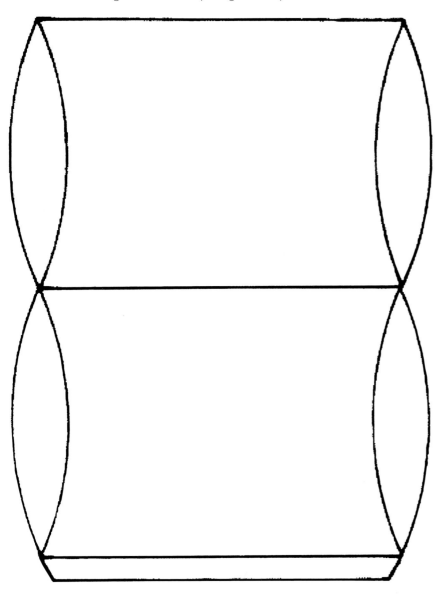

## SUPPLIES

**Glues:**

Permanent spray adhesive

Double-sided adhesive tape

**Papers:**

White cardstock

Magazine page with no text

**Tools:**

Scissors

Craft knife

Bone folder or scoring tool

Cutting mat

Pillow box template

## INSTRUCTIONS

1. Tear out a colorful magazine page that
   has no written text or advertising.
2. Spray cardstock with adhesive.
3. Tear magazine page into three or four
   pieces. Lay each piece on the cardstock,
   keeping the edges in line but allowing a
   1/4" gap to expose the tear. Smooth with
   fingers to push out any air bubbles.
4. Lay cardstock on cutting mat. Using the
   template, cut and score to create a pillow
   box.
5. Close side of box with double-sided
   adhesive tape. ❏

# Dream Big Card

Encourage the dreamer in all of us with this pop-up card filled
with good wishes and cutout flowers. You could easily personalize
this card to give a lift to a special dreamer you know.

## SUPPLIES

**Glues:**

Permanent spray adhesive

Laminating machine, adhesive runner

Adhesive dots

**Papers:**

White cardstock

Scrapbook papers, 2 patterns

Scrapbook papers, 2 solid colors that complement patterned papers

**Embellishments & Trims:**

Alphabet stickers, 2 sizes

3 heart-shaped brads

Daisy cutouts

**Tools:**

Scissors

Decorative edge scissors, scallop cut

Decorative edge scissors, zigzag cut

Craft knife

Bone folder or scoring tool

Metal edge ruler

Cutting mat

Pop-up template *(from "You're Invited Invitation" project)*

*Optional* Die-cut machine with daisy-shaped die

## INSTRUCTIONS

1. Cut white cardstock to a size that will accommodate the pop-up insert. Score and fold in half.

2. With scallop decorative scissors, cut a piece of scrapbook paper 1/2" smaller all around than front of card. Adhere to center of card front with adhesive runner.

3. Adhere larger alphabet stickers to spell "Remember. . ."

4. Cut two large and two small daisies from the solid color papers. Attach to card front with adhesive dots, allowing some petals to overlap edge of card.

5. Place one brad in each daisy center.

6. Adhere a sheet of scrapbook paper with spray adhesive to inside of card.

7. Place card on cutting mat. Using the craft knife and ruler, carefully trim daisy petals and inner lining flush with edge of card.

8. Trim another sheet of scrapbook paper 1/2" smaller than size of card. Edge with zigzag decorative scissors.

9. Place pop-up template over trimmed paper. (see "You're Invited Invitation" project for template) Cut and score according to template directions.

10. Adhere the pop-up inside the card with adhesive runner.

11. Cut five small daisies from each solid color paper. Attach background daisies to pop-up steps with adhesive dots.

12. Use the smaller alphabet stickers to spell out one word of "Dream Big Dream Far" on each of four of the foreground daisies. Attach a brad to the center daisy.

13. Attach foreground daisies to background daisies with adhesive dots. ❏

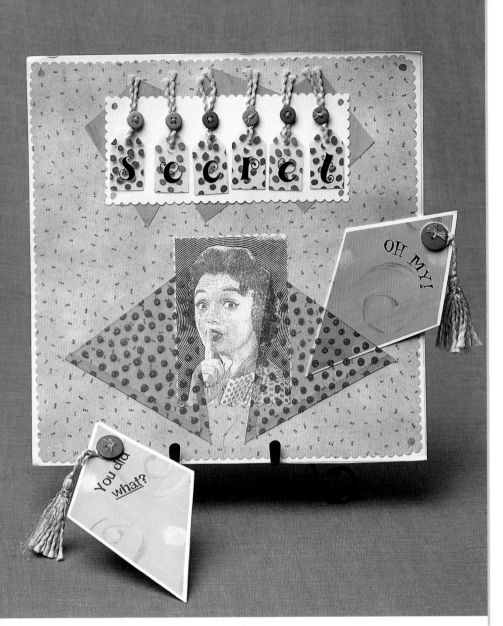

# Secrets Scrapbook Page

Glue see-through polka dot pockets on this scrapbook page to contain tiny "secret" journals for recording especially giggly events that you don't ever want to forget.

## SUPPLIES

**Glues:**

Laminating machine pressed adhesive runner (or spray adhesive)

Adhesive tape runner

Adhesive dots

Double-sided adhesive tape

**Papers:**

3 sheets white scrapbook paper, 12" x 12"

2 sheets contrasting scrapbook paper, 12" x 12"

1 sheet transparent plastic, 12" x 12"

**Embellishments & Trims:**

2 large buttons, 3/4" size

6 medium buttons, 1/2" size

Alphabet stickers

Yarn, coordinating colors of your choice

**Other Supplies:**

Rubber stamp, vintage girl with secret

Black inkpad

**Tools:**

Scissors

Decorative edge scissors, scallop cut

Tag punch, 1" wide size

Hole punch

Silver paint pen

Tassel tool – or cut your own from cardboard

## Patterns
Enlarge @200% for actual size.

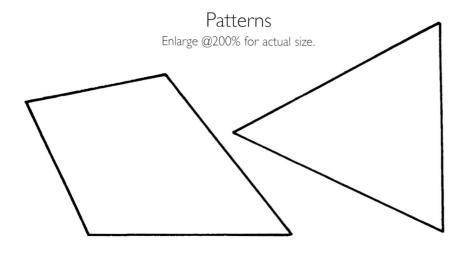

# INSTRUCTIONS

1. Cut edge of scrapbook paper with decorative scissors on all sides. Place through laminating machine-pressed adhesive runner. Adhere to a sheet of white cardstock.
2. Cut 3 uneven blocks of contrasting paper. Adhere to title area with tape runner.
3. For title area, Cut 7-1/4" x 3-1/4" white rectangle with decorative scissors. Adhere over blocks with tape runner.
4. Punch out 6 tags from transparent plastic. Apply alphabet stickers to spell "secret". Draw polka dots on back sides of tags with silver paint pen. Punch holes in tags. Thread yarn through holes and adhere to the title area with adhesive dots. Adhere medium sized buttons over yarn with adhesive dots.
5. Stamp girl image onto white cardstock. Cut out with decorative scissors. Glue to bottom center of page with machine pressed adhesive runner.
6. Following the pattern, cut two triangle pockets from transparent plastic. Draw polka dots with silver paint pen. Adhere to page with double-sided adhesive tape.
7. Following the pattern, cut white cardstock to form two diamond-shaped cards. Cut diamond shapes from scrapbook paper, 1/4" smaller, and adhere to diamond-shaped cardstock with adhesive runner. Add words with alphabet stickers.
8. Make two 1" tassels with yarn. *(See box)* Glue tassel and large button to each diamond-shaped card with adhesive dots. Place inside triangular pockets.

## How to Make a Tassel

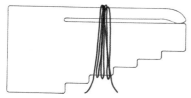

1. Wind yarn and fibers around the tassel tool at the length you desire. Continue winding until the tassel is as full as you want it to be. If you prefer, you may cut a piece of sturdy cardboard to the length of the tassel. Wind yarn around the cardboard.

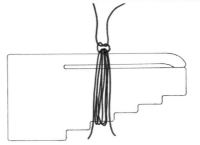

2. Tie a separate length of yarn around the top of the tassel, by slipping the yarn through the top loops of the tassel. Tie securely, leaving enough yarn for a hanger.

3. Bind the neck of the tassel by threading another length of yarn through the slot, around the neck of the tassel. Tie the yarn securely, leaving the ends to hang within the tassel. If you are using cardboard, slip the yarn off the cardboard and bind the top with yarn, tying in a knot.

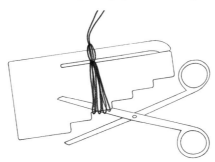

4. Cut the bottom of the tassel away from the tool, by slipping scissors through the loops to cut. Pull the finished tassel down the neck of the tool, gently flexing the tool to release the finished tassel. If you are using cardboard, cut the loops at the bottom of the tassel. Trim the ends evenly across the bottom.

# Let's Dance Party Favors

Turn polka dot paper into party favors that will make your guests want to dance! Fill the miniature high-heeled shoes with candy and place a note inside the purse for a treat they will be happy to take home.

## SUPPLIES

**Glues:**

Permanent spray adhesive

Adhesive dots

Double-sided adhesive tape

**Papers:**

3 sheets white cardstock

Polka dot gift wrap

Striped gift wrap

White embroidered scrapbook paper

**Embellishments & Trims:**

Paper twist or cording, 12"

Black feather boa

1 large button for purse

2 matching buttons for shoes

**Tools:**

Scissors

Craft knife

Bone folder or scoring tool

Cutting mat

Metal edge ruler

Tracing paper & transfer paper

Purse & shoe templates or use patterns
  provided

## INSTRUCTIONS

1. Trace patterns for purse and shoes onto tracing paper.
2. With spray adhesive, adhere striped gift wrap to one side, and polka dot gift wrap to the other side, of two sheets of white cardstock.
3. Place one glued sheet on cutting mat. Transfer shoe pattern to paper. Using the craft knife, cut outline of shoe, then cut along lines that separate sole and heel from sides of shoe. Finish cutting out the shoe.
4. Score along the fold lines.
5. Fold inward along scored lines to form shoe. Adhere with adhesive dots. Cut out and assemble second shoe.
6. Cut small tufts from boa. Adhere to toes of shoes with adhesive dots. Attach matching buttons with

adhesive dots in centers of tufts.
7. Adhere polka dot gift wrap to remaining sheet of white cardstock with spray adhesive.
8. Place glued paper on cutting mat. Transfer purse pattern to paper. Using a craft knife, cut around the outline of the purse. Score along the fold lines.
9. Fold inward along scored lines to form purse. Adhere with double-sided adhesive tape.
10. Cut white embroidered paper to fit purse flap. Adhere to purse with double-sided adhesive tape.
11. Attach large button to purse flap with adhesive dot. To create a handle, attach cording to back of purse with adhesive dots.
11. Tuck netted candies or small gifts inside shoes if desired. ❑

## Purse Template
Enlarge pattern to size of your choice.

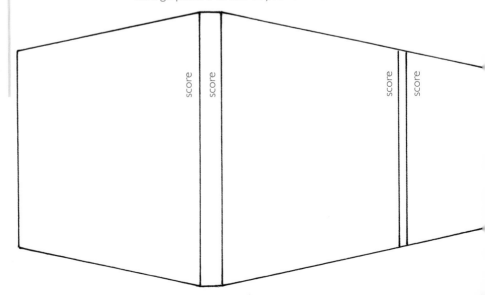

# Let's Dance
## Shoe Templates
### Actual Size

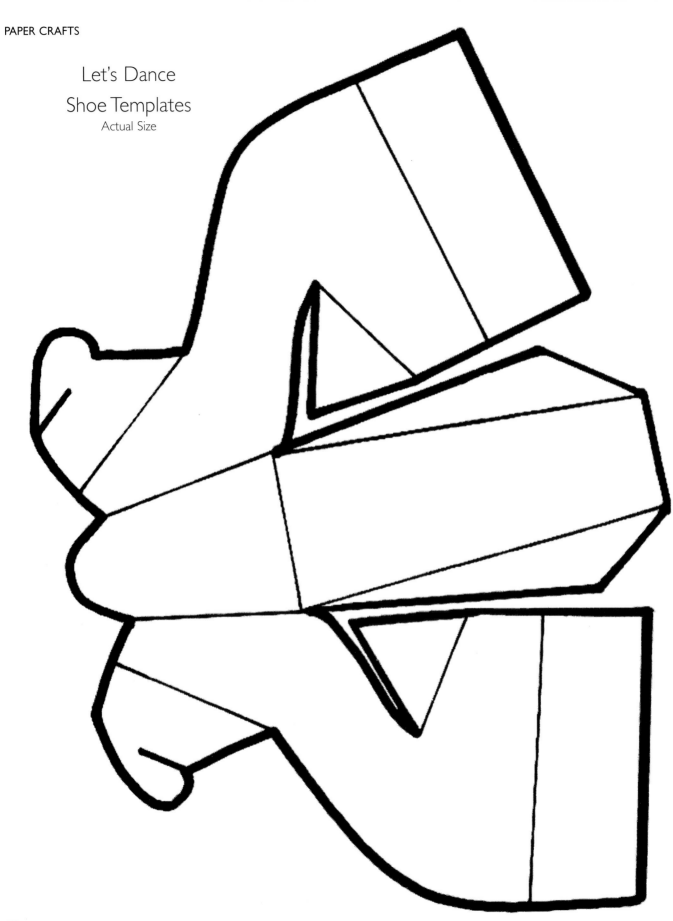

Spout

Tea Time Templates

Instructions begin on page 52.

## SUPPLIES

**Glues:**

Permanent spray adhesive

Adhesive dots

Double-sided adhesive tape

Scrapbooking tape

**Papers:**

3 sheets white cardstock

3 sheets coordinating scrapbook paper

**Embellishments & Trims:**

Assorted beads

Bead with flat back for gift box flap

Large round bead for teapot lid, approx. 12mm

2 flat buttons for teapot lid, 3/4" and 1/2"

Sticker sayings

Sticker face

Artistic wire

Pin back

3 eye pins, 1-1/2"

3 jump rings

*Optional:* Sticker floral decorations

*Optional:* Teapot and pillow box templates or use patterns provided

**Tools:**

Scissors

Craft knife

Bone folder or scoring tool

Cutting mat

Metal edge ruler

Needle nose pliers

# Tea Time Invitation & Favors

Make your next tea party a memorable occasion with these darling paper favors. Delight your guests by hiding aromatic tea bags inside the paper teapot, and a whimsical pillow box pin inside the gift box.

## INSTRUCTIONS

**Teapot:**

1. Adhere a sheet of scrapbook paper to a sheet of cardstock with spray adhesive.
2. Place paper on cutting mat. Trace teapot template pattern from book onto tracing paper or use a purchased teapot template. Lay onto the cardstock. Cut along outline with craft knife. Score along fold lines. Fold inward along scored lines to form teapot. Adhere with double-sided adhesive tape, keeping top free to open and close.
3. Cut spout out of leftover paper. Glue to pot with adhesive dots.
4. Punch a hole in center of top of teapot. Thread two buttons and a bead onto wire and insert into top of lid. Secure wire to inside of lid with scrapbooking tape.
5. Add a sticker saying to side of teapot. Place tea bags inside if desired.

**Gift Box:**

1. Adhere a sheet of scrapbook paper to a sheet of cardstock with spray adhesive.
2. Place paper on cutting mat. Use the pillow box pattern included with the "Let-r Rip Gift Boxes" project or use a purchased box template. Lay template or traced pattern over paper. Cut along outline with craft knife. Score along fold lines. Fold inward along scored lines to form pillow box. Adhere with double-sided adhesive tape, keeping one end free to open and close.
3. To make the flap, cut a triangle shape to fit the box.

4. String beads onto 4" of wire and insert into top edge of flap, securing underneath with tape. Attach a flat bead to the point with an adhesive dot.
5. Adhere flap to front of box with double-sided adhesive tape.
6. Embellish box with sticker sayings.

**Invitation:**

1. Adhere a sheet of scrapbook paper to a sheet of cardstock with spray adhesive.
2. Cut a piece 5" x 6". Score and fold in half.
3. String beads onto 5" of wire, leaving 1" clear at each end. Punch holes in card and thread wire through holes. Coil wire on each end to secure, as shown in the photo.
4. Embellish card with sticker sayings.

**Pillow Box Pin:**

1. Reduce the pillow box pattern or use the smallest size pillow box template. Assemble in the same manner as the large pillow box.
2. String beads onto wire, leaving 1" clear at each end. Punch two holes at top of box and thread beaded wire through holes. Secure ends inside box with scrapbooking tape.
3. Punch three holes at bottom of box.
4. Thread beads onto three eye pins. Loop both ends of eye pins. Attach through punched holes with jump rings.
5. Add sticker face to front of pin.
6. Attach pin back with double sided tape. ❏

# Zane's First Circle Book

Believe it or not, this circle book is made from paper bags! Celebrate any occasion with this sturdy and economical book that naturally creates pockets for photo discs, ticket stubs, trinkets, and mementos. Open out the pages and you have an instant table display to remind you of that special day.

## SUPPLIES

**Glues:**
Scrapbooking tape
Laminating machine pressed sticker adhesive
Adhesive dots
Paper glue
Double-sided adhesive tape

**Papers:**
2 large brown paper bags without printing
Assorted scrapbook papers

**Embellishments & Trims:**
Stickers – alphabets, sayings, pictures, etc.

Die cut shapes and words
Ribbons, trims, rick rack, etc.
Assorted buttons
Decorative stapler and staples
Metal clips
Brads

**Other Materials:**
Photographs
Mementos such as photo discs, tickets stubs, trinkets, etc.

**Tools:**
Scissors

## INSTRUCTIONS

1. Cut out two 12" diameter circles from flat sides of brown paper bags.
2. Fold each circle in half, then into quarters. See Fig. 1.
3. Unfold circles. Lightly pencil numbers 1, 2, 3, and 4 in the quarters of the first circle. Cut from the outside edge to the center along the fold line between section 1 and section 4. (See Fig. 1)
4. Lightly pencil numbers 5, 6, 7, and 8 in the quarters of the second circle. Cut from the outside edge to the center along the fold line between section 5 and 8. (See Fig. 1)
5. Lay the second circle on top of the first circle with cuts aligned. (See Fig. 2)
6. Fold back section 8 to reveal section 4. (See Fig 3)
7. Tape section 4 to section 5. (See Fig 4)
8. Starting with section 8, fold the sections back and forth to create a pie-shaped book. (See Fig 5)
9. When the book is folded, tape sections 1 and 8 together at the seam to complete. (See Fig 6) Trim edges evenly if needed.
10. Embellish the book with scrapbooking supplies, using the machine pressed sticker adhesive to run the trims through, for ease of adhering to the book.
11. Use the adhesive dots, glue, and tapes to adhere the smaller items to the pages.
12. Staple ribbon to form tabs on the edges of the pages.
13. Add photo cut-outs and adhere to pages with the machine pressed adhesive.
14. Insert photo disc and other mementos into the pockets.
15. Display the book by opening the pages and place on tabletop. ❏

Fig 1
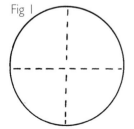

Fig 2
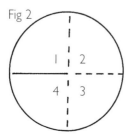

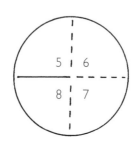

Fig 3
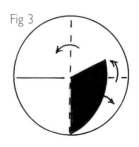

Fig 4

# CHAPTER 4

# Outdoor Living

When you make projects to be used outdoors, you want durable materials and adhesives that can stand up to the weather. Ice, snow, and rain are obviously challenging conditions, but so is ultraviolet light on those bright, sunny days. Look for adhesives that are UV-resistant and hold together regardless of drastic changes in temperature and humidity. You will enjoy making the outdoor decor projects in this chapter even more when you can be sure you have used the right glues. Keep the candle holders and clock under shelter (rain isn't good for wax and clockworks) but you can plant the bird feeders right out in the middle of the flower bed.

## Glues to Use

All purpose, super strength adhesive
Two-part epoxy

# Sundown Candle Keepers

Light up the patio or porch with these stylish candle keepers. Transform the saucer into a lid when you glue a wooden finial on top. Fill the pot with sand that safely holds a glimmering tea light candle when the sun goes down.

## INSTRUCTIONS

1. In a well-ventilated area, preferably outdoors, spray wooden balls and finial with red indoor-outdoor paint. Let dry.
2. Spray wooden balls and finial with red stained glass spray paint. Let dry thoroughly.
3. Stamp a design on front of clay pot with black permanent ink. Turn saucer upside down and stamp a design in the center. This will be the top of the lid.
4. Using a black marker, draw stripes and other designs on pot and saucer.
5. Glue wooden balls to bottom of pot for feet. Glue finial to center top of saucer. Let dry completely.
6. Cover hole in bottom of pot with duct tape on inside of pot.
7. Fill pot with sand and insert a tea light.
8. Add tassel to embellish the finial. ❏

## SUPPLIES

**Glues:**
All purpose, super strength adhesive
Duct tape

**Surface:**
5" clay bulb pot & saucer

**Embellishments & Trims:**
4 wooden ball feet, 1/2" size
1 wooden finial
Tassel, purchased or handmade with fibers of your choice *(See "How to Make a Tassel" in the "Secrets Scrapbook Page" project, Chapter 3.)*

**Paint:**
Red stained glass spray paint
Red indoor-outdoor spray paint

**Other Supplies:**
Rubber stamp of your choice
Permanent black ink pad
Sand
Tea light

**Tools:**
Metal edge ruler
Black permanent marker

# Time to Relax Tile Clock

It takes only a little time to make this handsome clock for outdoors. Choose a tile that coordinates with a covered sitting area, and simply glue stones and stamp messages of "peace" and "harmony" onto the face of your clock to remind yourself to relax and enjoy the view.

## SUPPLIES

**Glue:**
All Purpose, super strength adhesive

**Surface:**
Concrete tile

**Embellishments & Trims:**
Smooth, flat-bottomed stones

**Other Supplies:**
Permanent ink pad
Rubber stamps of your choice
Clock kit

**Tools:**
Drill & concrete bit to fit clock kit

## INSTRUCTIONS

1.  Drill a hole in center of tile to fit size of clock kit.
2.  Stamp images on face of tile.
3.  Glue stones around edge of tile.
4.  Insert clock kit. Anchor on back of tile with adhesive gel. Let dry. ❑

# Chiminea Mosaic Fountain

Turn a chiminea into a fountain. Cover the outside of the chiminea with broken dishes for a mosaic surprise. A miniature tea set added to the design gives it an unexpected whimsical touch.

## SUPPLIES

**Glues:**

All purpose, super strength adhesive

**Surface:**

Chiminea

**Embellishments & Trims:**

Broken ceramic and china dishes

Miniature tea set

**Other Supplies:**

Grout

Sponge & water

Hammer

Drill and drill bit

Fountain pump & plastic tubing, about 12" or more

Clay pot to house pump, (sized to turn upside down in the chiminea)

Sealer & brush

## INSTRUCTIONS

1. Seal the inside of the chiminea to enable you to add water for the fountain. Let dry.
2. Drill a hole in the back of the chiminea above water level, for the cord to pull through from the pump.
3. Break dishes into small pieces with a hammer. Glue broken dishes and miniature tea set to the front and sides of the chiminea using all purpose adhesive.
4. Apply grout according to package directions. Let dry.
5. Apply sealer to the outside of the pot and over the mosaics.
6. Break a small chip out of the lip of the clay pot.
7. Place the pump inside the bottom of the chiminea. Put clay pot over pump, upside down, pulling the cord through the hole. Pull the pump tubing up through the clay pot's drain hole.
8. Fill the rest of the chiminea with broken dishes, enough to cover the tubing.
9. Pour water into the chiminea until the pump is submerged. Plug into an outlet and enjoy! The water will cascade over the dishes, making a lovely tinkling sound. ❏

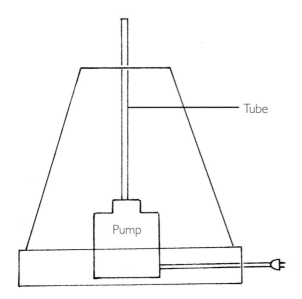

Tube

Pump

# Garden Glam Teacup Bird Feeders

Glam up your garden and surprise your feathered friends with clever feeders made with cups and saucers – or place tea lights inside glass cups to light a pathway or patio.

# SUPPLIES

**Glues:**

Two-part epoxy

All purpose, super strength adhesive

**Surface:**

Ceramic or glass cups and saucers

**Embellishments & Trims:**

Flat glass stones

Assorted buttons

Figurine

Beaded wire

**Other Supplies:**

Copper pipe, 3' long

Copper cap to fit pipe

Rubbing alcohol

Paper towel

Paper plate

**Tools:**

Craft stick

# INSTRUCTIONS

1. Wash, rinse, and dry cup and saucer. Wipe with alcohol and paper towel.
2. Glue cup to saucer with all purpose adhesive.
3. Embellish with buttons, stones, and figurine, attached with adhesive. Let set according to label instructions.
4. Mix two-part epoxy on paper plate with craft stick, following label instructions. Turn cup and saucer upside down. Apply epoxy in center of saucer bottom. Apply epoxy to copper cap. Press cap onto saucer. Let set according to epoxy label instructions.
5. Position copper cap on one end of copper pipe.
6. Wind beaded wire through cup handle and down length of pipe.
7. Push pipe into ground. Add birdseed and fresh water, or tea lights. ❏

# CHAPTER 5

# Glass Projects

Photos and glass, plastic and glass, collage and glass – with the right glue, you can adhere almost anything to almost anything else! These glass projects include whimsical breakfast dishes for kids; elegant, gold-bordered tree ornaments; and plates and platters that serve up holiday memories for the whole family.

## Glues to Use

Decoupage glue

Glass & metal glue

All purpose, super strength adhesive

Epoxy glue

# Doll it Up Candle Trio

Paper dolls have never been so much fun! Decoupage your favorites onto glass candle containers and add flirty tags for these glowing conversation starters.

## SUPPLIES

**Glues:**

Decoupage glue

White craft glue

**Surface:**

Candles in glass containers

**Decoupage Papers:**

Paper dolls *(color copies work well)*

**Embellishments & Trims:**

Self-adhesive acrylic tiles of your choice

Black cording

Black felt square

**Tools:**

Scissors

Disposable brush

## INSTRUCTIONS

*Use purchased paper dolls or color photo-copies, or print out paper doll images from sources on the internet. Remember: copy-righted materials may not be sold, but copied only for your personal use.*

1. Cut out paper dolls.
2. Glue doll cutouts around sides of containers with decoupage glue. Let dry.
3. Apply a thin layer of decoupage glue over paper. Be careful not to saturate paper, which may cause the ink to bleed. Let dry.
4. Tie cording around container, a safe distance from the candle flame.
5. Cut felt 1/4" larger than acrylic tiles. Glue ends of cord between tile and felt with white craft glue. Let dry. ❏

## SUPPLIES

**Glues:**

Non-toxic glass & ceramic glue, permanent and water resistant *(Some outdoor glues can be used.)*

**Surfaces:**

Glass bowls and tumblers

**Embellishments & Trims:**

Plastic figurines (frog and puppy used)

Alphabet stickers or glass paint

**Other Supplies:**

Rubbing alcohol

Paper towels

**Tools:**

Metal file

# Peek-A-Boo Breakfast Sets

Next time you set the breakfast table for the kids, play "Peek-a-Boo" with cheerful puppy and frog figurines glued to the tumblers and bowls. Choose **non-toxic, dishwasher safe glue** for a kid-friendly project that will delight everyone. The stickers are fun for a special day, but are not permanent.

## INSTRUCTIONS

1. Wash, rinse, and dry glass bowls and tumblers. Wipe glass with alcohol and paper towel.
2. File a groove in the bottom of a frog or a puppy, so the groove fits over the lip of the bowl.
3. Glue figurines onto lips of bowls with non-toxic, dishwasher safe glue, following directions on label.
4. Glue a figurine in the bottom of each tumbler.
5. Add alphabet stickers if desired. You can also paint names or sayings on the bowls and glasses using permanent glass paint. ❏

# A Glass Act Canister Set & Tray

Serve up some style on this silver tray! Fill the canisters with treats after you glue on acrylic tiles. Who knew you could use scrapbooking tiles this way?

## SUPPLIES

**Glues:**

All purpose, super strength adhesive

**Surfaces:**

Glass canisters

Metal tray

**Embellishments & Trims:**

Acrylic tiles

Flat glass stones

**Other Supplies:**

Rubbing alcohol

Paper towel

## INSTRUCTIONS

1. Wash, rinse, and dry glass canisters and tray. Wipe surfaces with alcohol and paper towel.
2. Lay out tiles and stones in desired arrangement.
3. Glue tiles and stones to canisters and tray, following directions on label. Let dry completely. ❑

## SUPPLIES

**Glues:**
Decoupage or laminate glue

**Surfaces:**
Glass plates & platter *(plastic works as well)*

**Decoupage Papers:**
Color copies of photos *(do not use glossy paper)*

Decorative paper – gift wrap, tissue, napkins, Christmas cards, wallpaper, calendars, art prints, or packaged papers

**Other Supplies:**
Disposable plate
*Optional:* Spray sealer, clear

**Tools:**
Scissors
Disposable brush

### PattieWack Pointer:

What a super idea for the holidays: start a family tradition with a platter for each year, adding the date with a metallic paint pen. Another great idea is to let the kids make their own plates for a very special holiday dinner. Personalize plates with the guests' names and photos. After dinner, send them home as party favors!

# Christmas Collage Plates & Platter

Capture the candid moments of family holidays as you glue photos onto these glass plates and platter. They are ready to serve up goodies or to make a gorgeous display of Christmas colors on the mantel.

## INSTRUCTIONS

1. Cut backgrounds away from figures on copied photos to use as focal point on dish. Glue to back of dish using decoupage glue and disposable brush.
   Be careful not to get glue on plate where plate is clear. Let dry.
2. Glue on paper, patchwork of tissue or napkins, cutouts, and other images, layering over the photos.
3. Apply an additional coat of glue over entire back of plate. Let dry.
4. Spray sealer on back of plate if not using laminate glue. Let dry. ❏

# Heirloom Tree Ornaments

Create cherished ornaments from heirloom photos that bring back golden memories of family holidays long ago.

## SUPPLIES

**Glues:**
Decoupage or laminate glue
Dimensional foiling glue
All purpose, super strength adhesive gel

**Surface:**
Sheets of clear glass *(or glass shapes)*

**Decoupage Papers:**
Color copies of photos *(do not use original photos)*

**Embellishments & Trims:**

| | |
|---|---|
| Crafting foil | Jewelry clutches |
| Jump rings | Chain |
| Charms | Gold ribbon |

**Other Supplies:**
Waxed paper

**Tools:**

| | |
|---|---|
| Protective eye wear | Glass cutter |
| Needle nose pliers | Scissors |
| Disposable brush | |

## INSTRUCTIONS

1. Wearing eye protection, use a glass cutter to cut glass into pieces that fit the photos.
2. Glue copies of photos face down on the glass with decoupage or laminate glue, applied with the disposable brush. Apply a coat of glue to backs of photocopies. Let dry.
3. With needle nose pliers, pry the pointed end of a clutch open. (Clutches are made to hold cording for necklaces, but they work well for this technique.) Glue clutch to one side of ornament with adhesive gel, fitting the edge of the glass into the clutch. Repeat on other side of ornament. Add more clutches to bottom of ornament if you want to add charms. Let dry.
4. Apply foiling glue along the edges of the piece, covering sharp edges of glass. Lay on waxed paper to dry until glue is clear. The glue will remain tacky after it turns clear.
5. Press dull side of crafting foil against glue, burnishing it with your finger. Peel away plastic backing to reveal the foil. Repeat until all the glue is foiled.
6. Attach jump rings to clutches on ornaments. Attach charms. Tie ribbons. ❏

69

# CHAPTER 6

# Jewelry & Gems

When you can make your own jewelry, you will always have the perfect adornment for any outfit. Jewelry makes great gifts, too. You will be inspired by the variety of available beads, gems, and crystals as well as gold and silver jewelry findings. Jewelry glues are strong and easy to use, so it's time to add some sparkle to your crafts.

## Glues to Use

Jewel glue
All purpose, super strength adhesive gel
Decoupage or laminate glue
White craft glue
Paper glue, (archival quality photo-safe glue)
Dimensional foiling glue
Double-sided adhesive tape

# An Eye on Design Pendant

Ordinary glass stones become extraordinary when you glue them over a fascinating image such as a bare tree branch, a striking graphic design, or a mysterious eye. Oh my!

## SUPPLIES

**Glues:**
All purpose, super strength adhesive gel

**Surface:**
Transparent glass stones, flat on one side

**Embellishments & Trims:**
Images – magazine clippings, photos, etc.
Silver wire, 22 gauge
Jump rings
Necklace – cording, velvet rope, or chain

**Tools:**
Scissors
Pencil
Needle nose pliers

## INSTRUCTIONS

1. Lay glass stone over image to find the most desirable spot. Trace with a pencil and cut out.
2. Glue image to flat side of stone, sealing edges. Let dry.
3. Cut wire 2" long. Coil ends and make a loop in the center. Glue to back of pendant. Let dry completely.
4. Attach pendant to necklace with a jump ring. ❏

## SUPPLIES

**Glues:**

Decoupage or laminate glue

All purpose, super strength adhesive gel

Dimensional foiling glue

**Surface:**

Pane of clear glass *(or glass shapes)*

**Embellishments & Trims:**

Color copies of photos *(do not use
 original photos)*

Crafting foil

Jewelry clutches

Jump rings

Charms of your choice

Jewelry findings – chains, bracelets, pin
 backs, earrings, etc.

**Other Supplies:**

Sealable plastic bag, larger than the
 pane of glass

Thick towel

Waxed paper

**Tools:**

Protective eye wear

Hammer

Scissors

Disposable brush

# Baby Face
# Broken Glass Jewelry

These charming shards start out as a full pane of glass. Smash it with a hammer, then choose pieces that turn favorite photos into amazing jewelry with glues, findings, and metallic foil edges. Oh, baby!

## INSTRUCTIONS

1. Wearing eye protection, place glass inside plastic bag. Lay on top of towel. Tap center with a hammer to break into triangular pieces. Select suitable pieces for jewelry charms and carefully remove from bag. Seal bag and discard unused glass, out of reach of children.

2. Glue copies of photos face down on the glass with decoupage or laminate glue, applied with the disposable brush. Apply a coat of glue to backs of copies. Let dry.

3. With needle nose pliers, pry the pointed end of a clutch open. (Clutches are made to hold cording for necklaces, but they work well for this technique.) Glue clutch to one side of glass charm with adhesive gel, fitting edge of glass into the clutch. Repeat on other side of charm. Add more clutches to bottom of charm if you want to add dangles. Let dry.

4. Apply foiling glue along edges of piece, covering all sharp edges of glass. Lay on waxed paper to dry until glue is clear. The glue will remain tacky after it turns clear.

5. When foiling glue has turned clear, press dull side of crafting foil against glue, burnishing it with your finger. Peel away plastic backing to reveal foil. Repeat until all the glue is foiled.

6. Attach jump rings to clutches to attach to necklaces, bracelets, and earrings. ❑

# Broken Treasures Jewelry Collection

Don't cry over Grandmother's broken china! Turn it into cherished
heirloom jewelry that you can wear proudly in her honor. You could also
go on the hunt for vintage dishes to break into gorgeous china charms.

# SUPPLIES

**Glues:**

Dimensional foiling glue

Jewel glue

**Surface:**

China plate(s) or fragments

**Embellishments & Trims:**

Crafting foil

Jewelry clutches

Jewelry findings – eye pins, jump rings,
  pin backs, chains, etc.

Assorted beads

Charms of your choice

**Other Supplies:**

Plastic bag

Thick towel

Waxed paper

**Tools:**

Protective eye wear

Hammer

Round-nosed pliers

# INSTRUCTIONS

1.  Wearing eye protection, place a thick towel on work surface, and put china
    plate into plastic bag. Use hammer to break dish into small pieces appropriate
    for jewelry.
2.  Select suitable pieces of broken china and carefully remove from bag.
3.  For a brooch, glue a pin-back to back of china with jewel glue. Let dry.
4.  For charms, flatten clutches with pliers and glue to back of china. Let dry.
5.  Cover all edges of broken china with foiling glue. Lay on waxed paper to dry
    until glue is clear. The glue will remain tacky after it turns clear.
6.  When foiling glue has turned clear, press dull side of crafting foil against glue,
    burnishing it with your finger. Peel away plastic backing to reveal foil. Repeat
    until all the glue is foiled.
7.  Thread beads onto eye-pin and bend wire with pliers to make a loop. Attach to
    clutches on backs of china pieces where desired, or attach chains and charms
    for necklaces. ❏

# Dragonfly Pendant

A burnt brown bag emerges as a beautiful dragonfly, after you cut out the wings, cover them with glue, and hold them over a candle in this amazing craft technique. You won't believe your eyes!

## SUPPLIES

**Glue:**
White craft glue, thick type

**Surface:**
Heavy-weight brown paper bag

**Embellishments & Trims:**
T-pin, 1-1/2"
Glass beads (no plastic), graduated sizes, for body
Glass bead (no plastic), for head

Jump ring
Rub-on metallic wax finish, gold
Beaded necklace

**Other Supplies:**
Candle
Soft cloth

**Tools:**
Scissors
Round nose pliers

## INSTRUCTIONS

1. Cut bottom away from paper bag. Fold bag in half and cut out wing shapes to represent the dragonfly wings, so that you have two layers.
2. Place beads on T-pin, to make body and tail of dragonfly, leaving room for wings and head bead.
3. Spread glue over one layer of wings. Place the T-pin across one layer of wings and place the other layer of wings on top, leaving the beaded end exposed for the dragonfly tail. Press wings together with your fingers to ensure good contact with glue. Let dry.
4. Place a larger bead for dragonfly head on T-pin above wings. Loop end of wire with pliers.
5. Light the candle. Cover wings on both sides with craft glue, being certain that every part of the paper is covered with a heavy layer of glue.
6. Hold the body of the dragonfly and pass the wings over the candle flame until all of the glue turns black. The glue will wrinkle and bubble, causing a veined effect to form on the wings.
7. When all of the glue has been burned to a black color, blow out the candle. Let glue dry completely.
8. Polish wings with a soft cloth. Burnish wings with rub-on metallic wax finish.
9. Attach dragonfly to necklace with a jump ring. ❏

## SUPPLIES

**Glue:**
All purpose, super strength adhesive

**Surface:**
Metal burner cover (large)

**Embellishments & Trims:**
12 jeweled pins and brooches

**Other Supplies:**
Clock kit

**Tools:**
Drill and drill bits
Wire cutters

# Days Gone By Clock

Instead of hiding forgotten brooches and pins in a
drawer, take them out to star in this timeless display.
Would you believe this gleaming clock started out
as a burner cover for the kitchen stove?

## INSTRUCTIONS

1. Drill a hole in center of burner
   cover, same size as clock kit stem.
2. Assemble clock kit. Adhere to center back of burner cover all purpose
   adhesive gel. Let set according to
   directions on glue label.
3. Snip backs off pins and brooches
   with wire cutters. Arrange on clock
   face as desired.

4. Glue jewelry to clock face with
   adhesive gel. Let dry completely. ❏

## SUPPLIES

**Glue:**
Paper glue (archival quality photo-safe)

**Surface:**
Postage stamp of your choice

**Papers:**
Heavy cardstock
Scrapbook paper in coordinating color

**Embellishments & Trims:**
Crystals
Jump rings
Ribbon for necklace
*Optional:* Wire and beads

**Other Supplies:**
Pour-on high gloss resin & hardener kit
Small disposable cup & craft stick
Paper plate
Disposable support, such as a small hairspray cap
Petroleum jelly

**Tools:**
Scissors
Hole punch
Craft knife
Needle nose pliers

# Mr. Postman Stamp Necklace

Going to the post office will inspire you to get creative when you see this pretty necklace made from Audrey Hepburn collectors' stamps. You can turn any stamp or paper image into a work of wearable art with high gloss resin and a little glue.

## INSTRUCTIONS

1. Glue postage stamp to scrapbook paper. Trim 1/4" out from edge of stamp to create face of pendant.
2. Trace around pendant onto heavy cardstock and cut out. Repeat so that you have two cardstock cutouts.
3. Glue cardstock cutouts together. Glue pendant on top of cardstock. Let dry.
4. Punch a hole at top of pendant for jump ring. Punch a hole at bottom of pendant if you plan to add a dangle of wire and beads.
5. Rub petroleum jelly on top of a disposable support, such as a small hairspray cap. Set on center of paper plate. (Be careful to place the plate in a level and secure place for overnight drying.) Place pendant on top of support.
6. In disposable cup, mix resin and hardener according to directions on label. Pour over pendant until it covers the edges. Level resin with edge of craft stick. Gently blow on resin to release any bubbles.
7. Drop crystals into the resin after it begins to harden. Let dry overnight.
8. Re-punch holes in pendant. Trim away excess resin on back of pendant with craft knife.
9. Attach a jump ring to top of pendant. Create a necklace by threading ribbon through the jump ring.
10. Attach a jump ring to bottom of pendant to add wire and beads for a decorative dangle, if desired. ❏

# Necktie Makeovers – Evening Bags

Instructions on page 80

# Necktie Makeovers
# Evening Bags, Watchbands
# & Belts

You might not recognize that old tie after you give it
a makeover and turn it into a jeweled evening bag,
coin purse, watchband, or perhaps a belt!

## SUPPLIES

**Glues:**

Jewel glue

Fabric glue

Double-sided adhesive tape

**Surfaces:**

Neckties

**Embellishments & Trims:**

Your choice of trims such as sequin trim,
pompom trim, beaded fringe, etc.

Appliqués

Your choice of cabochons, gems, jewels,
rhinestones, etc.

D rings for belts and watchbands

Jeweled chains for shoulder straps on bags

**Tools:**

Chalk

Scissors

Straight pins

Clothespins

Crafting foam work mat

Needle & thread

## INSTRUCTIONS

**Monogram Belt:**
*Best for ties with overall patterns.*
1. Lay the tie on a piece of craft foam.
   Draw initial on bottom of tie with chalk
   to create a guideline.
2. Place a line of glue on guideline.
3. Lay sequin trim into the wet glue, pinning through tie into foam as you go.
4. Finish ends of sequin trim by adhering a
   cabochon over ends with a drop of glue
   to hold in place.
5. Let glue set. Pull out pins and wipe clean
   before glue dries completely.
6. Let the necktie dry overnight.

7. Measure the jeweled tie around your waist and cut off small end of tie to fit. Slip two D-rings over small end and fold back the fabric. Turn under 1/2" and adhere with fabric glue. Hold with clothespins until glue dries.

## Rhinestone Belt:

*Best for ties with images to outline or embellish.*

1. Decide where the best accents of the design are on the tie, and lay out the rhinestones until you like the look.
2. Move rhinestones aside. Squeeze a small drop or line of gem glue onto tie. Place rhinestones into glue. Let tie dry overnight.
3. Measure jeweled tie around your waist and cut off small end of tie to fit. Slip two D-rings over small end and fold back the fabric. Turn under 1/2" and adhere with fabric glue. Hold with clothespins until glue dries.

## Evening Bag:

1. Fold wide end of tie up and over. Adjust until you decide on the right length for an evening bag. Cut off the tie.
2. Turn cut end over 1/2" and fold again, gluing into place with fabric glue. Clamp with clothespins until glue dries.
3. Adhere trims, gems, appliques, etc., with double-sided adhesive tape.
4. For a shoulder strap, sew the ends of a beaded chain or necklace to the bag with needle and thread.

## Watchband:

1. Thread small end of a tie through watch pins and place on wrist to measure the length needed to fit. Cut off the tie to measure.
2. Slip two D-rings over cut end and fold back. Turn under 1/2" and adhere with fabric glue. Clamp with clothespins until glue dries. ❑

# CHAPTER 7

# Fashions in a Flash

There's more to fashion than garments and accessories. It's all in your attitude! You'll know you're cool whether you're showing off unique funky flip flops or an extravagantly embellished denim jacket. No sewing required – fabric glues make it easy to create a whole new look for your wardrobe. These projects are ideal for teens to express their own personal style.

## Glues to Use

Fabric glue
Fabric applique glue
Napkin applique
Hot glue
Double-sided adhesive tape

# Runway Encore Denim Jacket

Give last season's denim jacket an encore by gluing fanciful trims and fabric to the yoke and cuffs. Trim the collar and pockets with gathered ribbon, and iron a felt design onto the back for a playful fashion that will deserve a round of applause.

## SUPPLIES

**Glues:**
Fabric glue

**Surface:**
Denim jacket

**Embellishments & Trims:**
1/2 yard decorative fabric
1 yard satin roses trim
1 yard gathered ribbon trim

Iron-on felt applique of your choice
Ornamental pin (*a beaded flower is shown in the photo*)

**Tools:**
Scissors
Iron & ironing surface
Straight pins
Pencil
Paper

## INSTRUCTIONS

1. Lay paper on jacket shoulders. Trace around neck, down to front pockets, and over shoulders across the back. Add 1/2" of ease on all sides of tracing to make a pattern for the yoke.
2. Using the pattern, cut a yoke out of decorative fabric.
3. Turn edges under 1/2" on all sides of yoke. Glue in place.
4. Lay fabric yoke on jacket. Pin in place, lining up with the shoulders, neck, and seam lines of the jacket. Glue edges of fabric to jacket on all sides, keeping edges smooth. Pin if needed until glue is set.
5. Make a pattern for the inside cuffs of sleeves by tracing around the jacket cuff and adding 1/2" of ease on all sides of the tracing.
6. Using the pattern, cut cuffs out of decorative fabric.
7. Turn edges under 1/2" on all sides of cuffs. Glue in place.
8. Glue cuffs into sleeves. Pin if needed until glue is set.
9. Glue satin roses trim to base of fabric yoke across front of jacket above the pockets, and across back of jacket, turning the ends under. Pin temporarily if needed until glue is set.
10. Glue gathered ribbon to edges of collar and to tops of pockets.
11. Adhere felt iron-on design to back of jacket, following directions on package.
12. Attach ornamental pin to front pocket. ❏

# Funky Flip Flops

Treat your toes to these fluffy flip flops, with comfy, yarn-covered straps and happy-go-lucky pompoms. You'll want to make several pairs in different colors, and more to give away.

## SUPPLIES

**Glue:**
Double-sided adhesive tape, super sticky

**Surface:**
Rubber flip flops

**Embellishments & Trims:**
Yarn, 1 skein each of basic wrapping colors of your choice
Multiple decorative yarns

**Other Supplies:**
20 gauge wire

**Tools:**
Scissors
Pompom tool – or cut your own from cardboard
Wire cutters

## INSTRUCTIONS

*Refer to pompom instructions on page 25*

1. Place double-sided tape along top of straps. Wrap yarn around straps to cover completely, securing ends of yarn in place with tape.
2. Add decorative yarn over the yarn-wrapped straps, securing ends in place with double-sided tape.
3. Make two 3" pompoms, wrapping yarn around pompom tool 50 times. To add multiple decorative yarns, simply wrap two strands at a time, wrapping a strand of yarn and a strand of decorative yarn together. Tie the middle with wire. Cut pompom loops and trim into a ball shape. Cut off ends of wire tie, and turn the ends back into the pompom.
4. Cut a 5" piece of wire. Attach pompom to flip flop with wire. Cut off ends of wire, and turn the ends back into the pompom. ❏

# Pick a Pocket Jeans Purse

Don't throw away those old jeans until you cut out the pockets, because you will love this snappy bag that takes only minutes to make.

## SUPPLIES

**Glue:**
Hot glue gun and fabric glue sticks

**Surface:**
Denim jeans pockets

**Embellishments & Trims:**
Iron-on applique of your choice
1-1/2 yards eyelash cording
Decorative button
Hook & loop closure
Yarn, color of your choice

**Other Supplies:**
Large rubber stamp of your choice
Black permanent ink pad

**Tools:**
Scissors
Iron & ironing surface
Tassel tool – or cut your own from cardboard

## INSTRUCTIONS

1. Cut pockets out of jeans, adding a 1" allowance around sides and bottoms of pockets. Cut along top edge of pockets, even with the edge. Completely cut away insides of pockets.
2. Stamp both pockets with large rubber stamp. Let dry completely.
3. Iron applique to front of one pocket, following directions on package.
4. With right sides facing, hot glue the 1" allowance on sides and bottoms of the two pockets together.
5. Fold pocket edges toward middle of purse and hot glue into place.
6. Turn purse right side out.
7. Hot glue cording to edges of purse, with cording ends touching at bottom of purse.
8. Make a tassel using the tassel tool. *(See "How to Make a Tassel" in the "Secrets Scrapbook Page" project, Chapter 3.)* Attach to bottom of purse. Glue decorative button to top of tassel.
9. Adhere hook and loop closure to opening of purse. ❑

## SUPPLIES

**Glues:**

Double-sided adhesive sheet

1/4" double-sided adhesive tape

**Surfaces:**

Hard-cover glasses case

Mirror compact

Wooden Buckle

**Embellishments & Trims:**

Assorted colored beads

Clear micro-mini beads

Crystals

Jeweled buttons

Plastic alphabet letters

**Other Supplies:**

Small bowl

**Tools:**

Pencil

Paper

Scissors

Craft knife

Wire cutters

*Optional:* Brayer

# Grand Illusions
# Mirror, Glasses Case & Belt

Create the illusion of intricate inlaid beadwork with masses of tiny beads. In reality, it takes very little time and effort to achieve a grand appearance on this chic belt buckle, glasses case, and mirror compact.

## INSTRUCTIONS

1. Trace around the glasses case, mirror compact, and buckle, onto a sheet of paper. Add 1/4" around the traced marking for the glasses case. Cut out patterns and place on each item to check the fit.
2. Using patterns, cut pieces from double-sided adhesive sheet.
3. Peel paper backing off double-sided adhesive pieces. Place onto items, easing corners into place on glasses case.
4. Place alphabet letters and crystals on buckle to spell "cute." Press pieces firmly into the adhesive.
5. Cut shanks off buttons with wire cutters. Place on mirror compact and glasses case. Add crystals if desired. Press the pieces firmly into the adhesive.
6. Pour clear micro-mini beads into a bowl. Dip items into bowl to cover adhesive with beads. Press beads firmly into adhesive with fingers or with a brayer. Repeat until adhesive is completely covered with beads. ❏

# Pooch Pouch Messenger Bag

See how easy it is to personalize your messenger bag with
a felt puppy appliqué and rick rack trims? Tie on matching
pompoms and you're ready to head out the door!

## SUPPLIES

**Glue:**

Fabric glue

**Surface:**

Purchased bag or tote

**Embellishments & Trims:**

Gem for eye

Rick rack trim

Yarn of your choice

**Other Supplies:**

Light brown felt square

Dark brown felt square

**Tools:**

Scissors

Pompom tool – or cut your own from cardboard

## INSTRUCTIONS

1. Enlarge or reduce pattern as desired to fit front of bag.
2. Cut puppy out of light brown felt, following the pattern. Cut ear out of dark brown felt.
3. Adhere felt pieces to front of bag with fabric glue.
4. Glue the eye gem to felt.
5. Glue rick rack trim to top flap of bag and to bottom edge, turning under the ends of the trim.
6. Make two pompoms. *(See "How to Make a Pompom" in the "Funky Flip Flops" project in this chapter.)*
7. Cut three pieces of yarn 10" long and braid them. Tie a pompom to each end of braid. Loop braid around handle of bag. ❏

## Pattern

Enlarge or reduce to fit size of your choice.

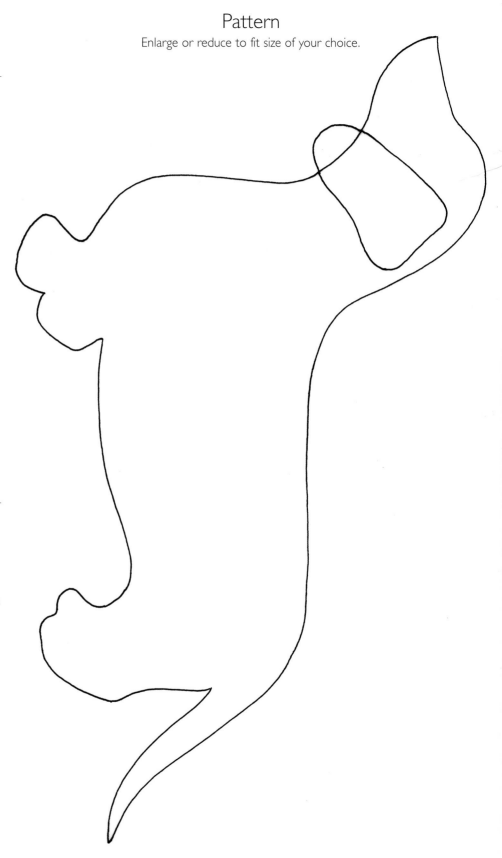

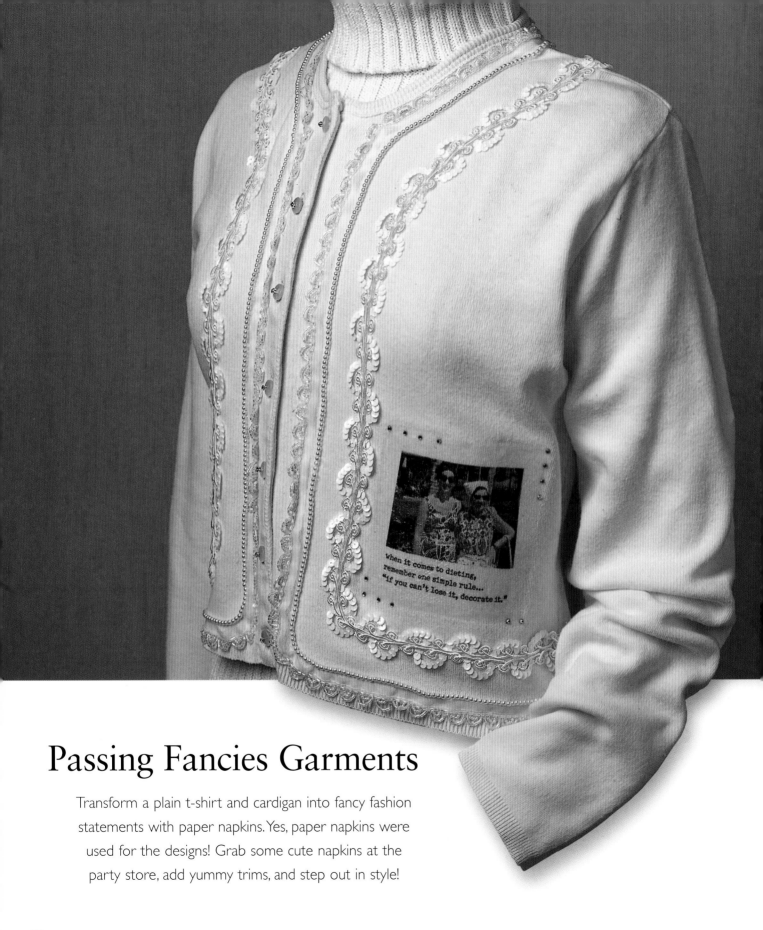

when it comes to dieting,
remember one simple rule...
"if you can't lose it, decorate it."

# Passing Fancies Garments

Transform a plain t-shirt and cardigan into fancy fashion
statements with paper napkins. Yes, paper napkins were
used for the designs! Grab some cute napkins at the
party store, add yummy trims, and step out in style!

# SUPPLIES

## Glues:

Fabric applique glue *(for napkins)*

Fabric glue

Jewel glue

## Surfaces:

*White or light-colored poly/cotton blend fabrics work best.*

T-shirt, laundered and pressed

Knit cardigan, laundered and pressed

## Embellishments & Trims:

Paper napkins of your choice

Crystals

Your choice – braid, strings of pearls, sequined trims, ribbons, satin roses, etc.

## Other Supplies:

Waxed paper

Disappearing ink pen

## Tools:

Scissors

Iron & ironing surface

Straight pins

Disposable brush

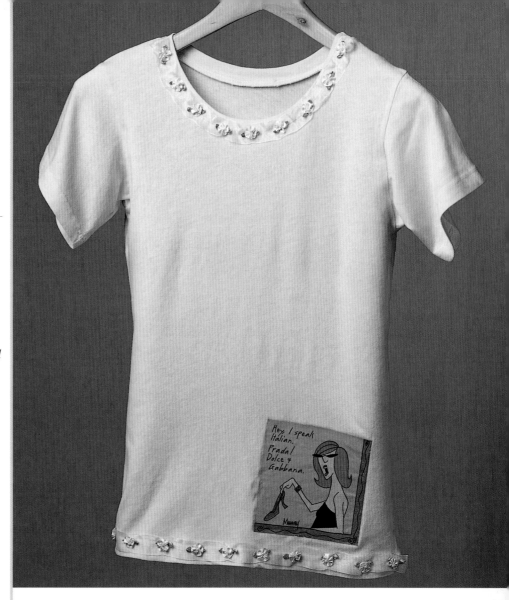

# INSTRUCTIONS

1. Cut designs from napkins. Separate plies, discarding all except the printed ply.
2. Place waxed paper under fabric before applying glue.
3. Position top ply of napkin on fabric. Outline with disappearing ink pen.
4. Remove napkin. Brush an even coat of fabric applique glue in outlined area. (The more glue you use, the stiffer the fabric will become.)
5. While wet, place napkin carefully onto the wet glue area. Delicately brush a layer of glue over the napkin, working from center to edges, to seal. Let dry flat.
6. Embellish the garment with trims along neckline, bottom, and any other area you desire, adhered with fabric glue. Hold trims in place with straight pins until glue sets. Remove and wipe pins before glue is completely dry.
7. Adhere crystals with jewel glue on buttons and as accents.
8. Let garment dry for 24 hours before wearing. Let dry 7 to 10 days before hand washing, laying flat to dry. ❑

# CHAPTER 8

# Have Glue Gun Will Travel

If you believe anything that stands still for five minutes can be embellished, the hot glue gun is for you! Hot glue is great for porous materials, such as wood, fabric, cardboard, and silk flowers, and it dries fast. The projects in this chapter show you how to organize your CDs and rubber stamps, cover a gift basket with corks, and make romantic floral accessories. Here's the ultimate recycling project – cover an old recliner with worn blue jeans.

## Glues to Use

Hot glue gun
Glue sticks
Fabric glue sticks

# Cube It CD Boxes

Make as many of these clever cubes as it takes to round up the CD's beside your computer or your stereo, and put an end to all that clutter. Choose fabrics to complement your decor, or go wild with animal prints.

## SUPPLIES

**Glue:**
Hot glue gun & glue sticks

**Surface:**
Foam core board, 1/4" thick

**Embellishments & Trims:**
Fabric – your choice

**Other Supplies:**
CD cover *(for measuring)*

**Tools:**
Scissors
Craft knife
Metal edge ruler

## INSTRUCTIONS

1. Using the CD cover for a pattern, cut 4 pieces of foam core board, for top, bottom & sides.
2. Cut one 5" x 5" square of foam core board, for back.
3. Glue top, bottom, and sides together. Adhere back to sides.
4. Cut fabric square 15" x 15".
5. Set cube in center of fabric square. Fold fabric neatly around box, as if gift wrapping it. Glue to sides of box.
6. Cut a strip of fabric for trim, if desired, 25" long x 3" wide.
7. Glue long edge of fabric strip to outside edges along opening of box.
8. Fold fabric over edge of box and glue into place inside box edges, to finish open side of cube. ❏

# Uncorked Basket & Coasters

Make this witty basket for newlyweds, or for a housewarming gift. Fill it with
wine, good eats, and two coasters. Don't forget to throw in a corkscrew!

## SUPPLIES

**Glue:**
Hot glue gun & glue sticks

**Surfaces:**
Wicker gift basket
2 ceramic tiles, 4"

**Embellishments & Trims:**
Corks
Assorted decorative studs

**Tools:**
Serrated knife
Cutting board
Wire pliers

## INSTRUCTIONS

1. Cut corks in half lengthwise with the serrated knife, on the cutting board. Holding corks with wire pliers makes this easier and safer. Cut enough corks to cover sides of basket and tops of tiles.
2. Glue cork halves to basket and tiles in a pleasing design.
3. Press decorative studs into corks as accents. ❏

# Lazy Daze
# Covered Recliner

Use this "in-jean-ious" idea to cover unsightly furniture with well-used blue jeans. It's perfect for a college dorm room, a first apartment, or a teen's bedroom.

## SUPPLIES

**Glue:**
Hot glue gun & fabric glue sticks

**Surface:**
Recliner or other upholstered furniture

**Other Supplies:**
Several pairs of old jeans

**Tools:**
Heavy-duty scissors

## INSTRUCTIONS

1. Cut legs off jeans. Set remaining upper portion of jeans aside.
2. Cut legs along inseams, then cut remaining denim into assorted smaller pieces to fit areas that need covering.
3. Lay pieces on furniture for placement in a patchwork style. When you have a pleasing arrangement, glue in place directly onto the furniture. Tuck under all edges of each piece and glue to give a finished edge. ❑

# Rose Petal Votives

Don't stop with roses! Just think how fantastic it would be to cover glass votives with daisies, tulips, or any flowers that bloom with silk petals.

## SUPPLIES

**Glue:**
Hot glue gun & glue sticks

**Surfaces:**
Glass votive holders
Large silk roses & leaves

**Other Supplies:**
Tea lights

**Tools:**
Scissors

## INSTRUCTIONS

1. Pull or cut silk rose apart, laying out pieces according to size.
2. Starting with largest petals, glue petals around sides of glass votive with as little glue as possible, arranging petals to look natural.
3. Glue leaves under rose petals, around base of votive.
4. Place tea lights in votives. ❏

# Isn't It Romantic?
# Wreath & Candle Holders

Cover an oval wreath with romantic silk hydrangeas to add
a delicate touch to a garden party, the mantel, or perhaps
the bedroom. It's even more lovely when you combine it
with flower petal packages crowned with candlelight.

## SUPPLIES

**Glue:**
Hot glue gun & glue sticks

**Surface:**
Round foam wreath, 18"
2 foam blocks, 5" x 5"

**Embellishments & Trims:**
Silk hydrangea bush
Silk rose petals, 1 box
5 yards toile ribbon, 2-1/2" wide

**Other Supplies:**
4 bamboo skewers
Heavy wire, for wreath hanger
Dripless taper candles

**Tools:**
Scissors
Serrated knife
Wire cutters
Pencil

## INSTRUCTIONS

**Wreath:**
1. To form an oval, cut wreath in half with serrated knife. Cut off a 3" section from both halves. Connect wreath halves with hot glue, holding in place by piercing through both pieces with bamboo skewers. Trim skewers even with wreath surface.
2. Cut all blossoms and leaves from the hydrangea bush.
3. Push pencil point into wreath foam. Glue a blossom into the hole. Cover entire front and all around wreath with blossoms.
4. Glue large leaves to cover back of wreath.
5. Form a hanger from wire. Attach to top back of wreath.

**Rose Petal Packages:**
1. Push candles into tops of foam blocks to mark their placement. Remove candles and set aside.
2. Glue overlapping petals to cover tops and bottoms of blocks.
3. Glue ribbon around blocks. Glue loops and tails of ribbon around candle holes in tops of blocks. Glue large hydrangea leaves between ribbon loops until nice and full.
4. Insert candles back into center tops of decorated blocks. ❏

# Pet Parade Pillow

Take control of all of those stuffed animals tossed around your child's room.
Corral them onto one giant pillow with a little hot glue.

## SUPPLIES

**Glue:**
Hot glue gun & glue sticks

**Surface:**
Pillow, 18" x 18"

**Other Supplies:**
Small stuffed animals, enough to
    cover front of pillow
*Optional:* Fiberfill

**Tools:**
Scissors

## INSTRUCTIONS

1. If some stuffed animals are heavy with
   plastic pellets, cut them open along the
   back, remove pellets, and re-stuff toys
   with fiberfill. Hot glue cut edges together. This will keep the pillow from being
   too heavy.
2. Lay stuffed animals on front of pillow for
   placement, all facing the same direction.
3. Glue stuffed animals to front of pillow. ❏

# Great Wall of Stamps Organizer

If you use thrift store frames, these organizers will make inexpensive, artsy conversation pieces, and show off your treasured rubber stamps at the same time.

## SUPPLIES

**Glue:**
Hot glue gun & glue sticks

**Surface:**
Picture frame *(no glass)*

**Other Supplies:**
Black foam core board, 1/4" thick, approximately twice as large as frame

**Tools:**
Craft knife
Metal edge ruler
Glass head straight pins
Wire cutters

## INSTRUCTIONS

1. Measure opening of frame. Cut foam core board the exact same size. This will be the back of the box.
2. Cut two pieces of foam core board, 1-1/4" wide, the length of the frame opening. Cut two pieces of foam core board, 1-1/4 inches wide, the width of the frame opening.
3. Place frame face down on work surface. Glue foam core board strips to inside opening of frame, along each side, where the glass would normally be placed. Glue corners together where they meet. This will make the sides of the box.
4. Glue back of box to sides to complete the box.
5. Turn framed box face up. Lay out your rubber stamps the way you would like for them to be arranged on shelves inside the box.
6. Cut 1-1/4" strips of foam core board, the width of the inside of the box. Place in box between rows of rubber stamps to make shelves. Glue to secure. ❑

# CHAPTER 9

# Home Décor Quickies

One of the best things about glue crafts is that you can quickly complete a project in time for a special event, or give your space a new look just because you're in the mood. Working while your inspiration is fresh is a lot of fun. These distinctive accessories will express your crafty personality all around your home.

## Glues to Use

White tacky craft glue
Permanent spray adhesive
Super-strength adhesive gel
Foiling glue
Hot glue gun & glue sticks
Adhesive dots

# Sojourns Poster Frame

Beach sand is the secret ingredient for this inviting frame. It's perfect for a poster or vacation photo that reminds you of a peaceful place and memories that make you smile.

## SUPPLIES

**Glue:**
White tacky craft glue

**Surface:**
Picture frame

**Paint:**
Beige spray paint
White webbing spray paint

**Other Supplies:**
Paper plate
Newspaper
Beach sand

**Tools:**
Disposable brush

## INSTRUCTIONS

1. Remove glass from frame.
2. In a well ventilated place, preferably outdoors, spray frame with two coats of beige paint. Let dry after each coat.
3. Lay frame face up on newspapers. With disposable brush, spread tacky glue over entire front of frame.
4. Sprinkle sand over glue to cover frame.
5. Spray frame lightly with webbing paint. Let frame dry thoroughly before replacing the glass. ❑

# Carpe Diem
# Lampshade & Message Board

Add a warm, inviting touch to this message board and lampshade with handmade papers and fabulous fibers. Spell out messages with alphabet tiles to inspire you to "seize the day."

## SUPPLIES

**Glues:**
Permanent spray adhesive
White tacky craft glue
Hot glue gun & glue sticks
Adhesive dots

**Surfaces:**
Lamp & flat-paneled lampshade
Picture frame
Cardboard cut to fit into frame

**Embellishments & Trims:**
Assorted yarns and fibers
Handmade paper, 2 large sheets
2 beads, for tassel
Wood candle cup with 1/2" hole, for tassel

Upholstery tacks
Flat head tacks
Wood alphabet tiles

**Paint:**
Color of your choice for candle cup

**Other Supplies:**
Batting

**Tools:**
Scissors
Pencil
Disposable brushes
Tassel tool – or cut your own from cardboard

## INSTRUCTIONS

**Lampshade:**
1. Trace around lampshade panel onto handmade paper. Cut out all panels.
2. Brush tacky glue onto lampshade. Adhere paper to shade. Let dry.
3. Hot glue twisted fibers around each section and around top and bottom of lampshade.

**Memo Board:**
1. Cut batting same size as cardboard. Adhere batting to cardboard with permanent spray adhesive.
2. Cut handmade paper same size as cardboard. Adhere to batting with permanent spray adhesive.
3. Crisscross flat fibers on board at 4" intervals. Hot glue in place on back of cardboard.
4. Hot glue board into frame.
5. Press upholstery tacks into message board at each intersection of fibers.
6. Adhere wooden alphabet tiles to flat head tacks with adhesive dots.

**Tassel on lampshade:**
1. Paint candle cup to complement fiber colors. Let dry.
2. Reserve 20" length of strong fiber or ribbon. Wind remaining fibers around 4" tier of tassel tool until full enough for tassel. Gather top of fibers and tie tightly with reserved 20" length. Trim bottom of tassel. *(See "How to Make a Tassel" in the "Secrets Scrapbook Page" project, Chapter 3.)*
3. Push tassel hanger through candle cup. Thread beads onto hanger. Tie to lamp.
❏

# Retro Raves
# Cup Candle Holders

Dress up these sassy candles with a retro flair that reminds us of a French dressing room. Glue melamine coffee cups on tops of wood candlesticks, and tie on polka dot bows to echo the black buttons glued to the cups.

## SUPPLIES

**Glues:**

All purpose, super strength adhesive gel
Adhesive dots

**Surfaces:**

2 coffee cups
2 wood candlesticks, glossy black finish
*(If you can't purchase painted candlesticks, simply paint wooden candlesticks as desired.)*

**Embellishments & Trims:**

Grosgrain ribbon, 1" wide, color to match cups with black polka dots, 1 yd.
Black buttons, varied sizes

**Other Supplies:**

Permanent black marker
Small rubber stamps
Black permanent ink pad
Black embossing powders
Rubbing alcohol
Paper towels
Tea lights

**Tools:**

Scissors
Heat gun

## INSTRUCTIONS

1.  Wash cups with soap and water, rinse, and let dry. Wipe cups with alcohol on a paper towel. Let dry.
2.  Stamp cups with permanent ink, sprinkle with black embossing powder, and apply heat until stamped design is embossed.
3.  Personalize with names or sayings written with a permanent black marker.
4.  Attach buttons with adhesive dots to outsides of cups in a polka dot style.
5.  Glue cups to tops of candlesticks with adhesive gel.
6.  Tie ribbon into bows on candlesticks.
7.  Place tea lights in cups. ❏

103

# Glittery Affirmations Box & Orbs

Inspirational affirmations have never been prettier. This would be an unusual centerpiece, or a cheerful daily reminder to play, jump, enjoy, create, and dance! You could easily style the box and orbs for the holidays, if you like.

## SUPPLIES

**Glues:**
Foiling glue
White tacky craft glue

**Surfaces:**
Wooden box
2" and 3" foam balls, as many as desired

**Paint:**
Purple paint (for box)

**Embellishments & Trims:**
Silver leaf sheets, 1 package
Purple glitter
Mini brads, 1 package (100 brads per package)
Alphabet brads
Acrylic alphabet stickers

Tassel, purchased or handmade with fibers of your choice *(See "How to Make a Tassel" in the "Secrets Scrapbook Page" project, Chapter 3, or "Terrific Tassels" in this chapter.)*

**Other Supplies:**
*Optional:* Fine grade sandpaper
Soft cloth
Waxed paper
Paper plates
Small bowl
Foam sheet

**Tools:**
Scissors
2 foam brushes
Craft sticks

## INSTRUCTIONS

**Silver Leafed Box:**
1. Sand wooden box if needed, and remove all traces of sanding dust. Paint with two coats of purple paint, drying after each coat.
2. Apply foiling glue with foam brush to top and sides of box. Let dry until clear.
3. Cut waxed paper the same size as silver leaf sheets.
4. Open silver leaf book and lay waxed paper over first sheet, pressing with your hand. Pick up the waxed paper, with the sheet of silver now stuck to it. Carefully lay silver leaf on box, lifting away waxed paper. Repeat until entire box is covered with silver leaf.
5. Burnish silver leaf onto box with a soft cloth, wiping away excess.
6. Apply acrylic alphabet stickers to box to spell "inspirational affirmations."
7. Attach tassel to lid of box.

**Affirmation Orbs:**
1. Pour tacky craft glue onto a paper plate. Pour glitter into a small bowl.
2. Spear a foam ball with a craft stick and cover ball with glue, using a foam brush. Dip ball into glitter to cover. Push craft stick into foam sheet to hold until dry. Cover all foam balls with glitter.
3. Press alphabet brads into glittery balls to spell words of affirmation. Press mini brads all over ball, 1" apart.
4. Place finished balls inside box. ❏

# Terrific Tassels

Tassels are terrific for decorating drapery pulls, drawer handles, doorknobs, or candlesticks, or for enhancing a pillow, a lamp, or a plush box. Combine colors, fibers, and embellishments as you wish. There's no wrong way to do this!

## SUPPLIES

**Glues:**
Hot glue gun & glue sticks

**Surface:**
Wood tassel finials *(with hole all the way through)*

**Embellishments & Trims:**
Yarn and coordinating fibers
Feathers
Pompom fringe
Assorted beads

**Paint:**
Acrylic paints, colors of your choice

**Tools:**
Brush for acrylic paints
Scissors
Tassel tool – or cut your own from cardboard
*Optional:* Drill & 1/4" drill bit

## INSTRUCTIONS

**Finials:**
1. If the finial doesn't have a hole all the way through, drill a hole for inserting the tassel.
2. Paint wood with acrylics according to the look you desire.
3. For peacock feather tassel, wrap a long feather around the finial. Secure with hot glue.
4. For polka dot tassel, glue pompom fringe around inside rim of finial before inserting tassel.

**Tassels:**
1. Wind yarn and fibers around tassel tool at desired tier. Continue winding until tassel is as full as you desire.
2. Tie a separate length of yarn around top of tassel, by slipping through loops at top of tassel. Tie securely, leaving enough yarn for a hanger.
3. Bind tassel by slipping another length of yarn through slot in tassel tool and tying around neck of tassel. Tie securely, leaving ends to hang within tassel. If you are using cardboard, slip yarn off cardboard and bind around neck with yarn, tying in a knot.
4. Cut bottom of tassel away from tassel tool, by slipping scissors through loops to cut. Pull finished tassel down neck of tool, gently flexing tool to release finished tassel. If you used cardboard, cut loops at bottom of tassel. Trim ends evenly across the bottom.
5. Insert tassel into finial, pulling ends of yarn hanger up through top of finial. Thread beads onto yarn hanger and push all the way down to meet top of finial. Place a dab of glue inside bead to hold tassel in place.
6. To add feathers, glue ends of feathers into the tassel fringe. ❏

# CHAPTER 10

# Decoupage

Take advantage of modern decoupage glues to bond and seal papers to surfaces in one easy step. Colorful printed images are all around us. If you tear interesting pages from magazines as you finish reading them, you will soon accumulate a library of eye-catching pictures. Copy photographs, collect paper napkins, or take a poster off the wall and give it a new career as surface decoration. Good sharp scissors are a must for trimming closely around the edges of complex images. Set your imagination free to combine unrelated images in unexpected ways to discover new themes.

## Glues to Use

Decoupage glue

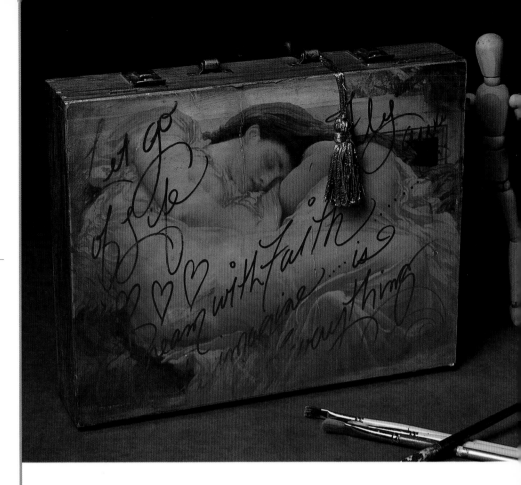

## SUPPLIES

**Glue:**
Decoupage glue

**Surface:**
Wooden attaché case

**Papers for Decoupage:**
Poster print of your choice

**Paint:**
Gold acrylic paint

**Other Supplies:**
Rub-on wax metallic finish, silver
Silver paint pen
Soft cloth

**Tools:**
Scissors
Foam brushes
Pencil
Straight pin

# Flaming June Artist's Attaché

Every artist needs a box like this one to fill with paint, palettes, canvas, and the hope of a masterpiece. Cover the lid of the box with an entire poster print, and write inspiring words with a silver paint pen.

## INSTRUCTIONS

1. Paint bottom and sides of box with gold acrylic paint. Let dry.
2. Lay box on poster to determine placement. Trace around box with pencil. Cut out poster on traced lines.
3. With a foam brush, apply a generous coat of decoupage glue to back of poster.
4. Apply a thin coat of decoupage glue to top of box. Let glue set for 5 minutes.
5. Lay poster over top of box, smoothing out the paper with your fingers.
6. Apply a generous coat of decoupage glue over entire poster. Swirl the glue and work it into the poster with your fingers, to create an antique look. Prick any bubbles with a pin and push them out with your fingers. Let dry overnight.
7. Write poetic, inspirational sayings on poster with silver paint pen.
8. Apply silver rub-on finish to edges of box, and buff with soft cloth. ❏

## SUPPLIES

**Glues:**

Decoupage glue

Hot glue gun & glue sticks

**Surfaces:**

Papier mache box

Plastic mask

**Papers for Decoupage:**

Paper napkins with Asian-inspired
theme

**Embellishments & Trims:**

Tassel, purchased or handmade with
fibers of your choice *(See "How to
Make a Tassel" in the "Secrets
Scrapbook Page" project, Chapter 3.)*

Assorted beads

**Paint:**

Black acrylic paint

Gold acrylic paint

**Other Supplies:**

Bamboo stick for mask stem

**Tools:**

3 disposable brushes

# Geisha Mystery Box & Mask

Create a dramatic composition for decoupage with
Asian inspired paper napkins. The matching mask and box
will add a mysterious, exotic accent to any room.

## INSTRUCTIONS

1. Separate napkin plies. Discard all
   but the printed top ply.
2. Arrange napkins on box lid and
   mask to determine best placement.
3. Apply one napkin at a time. With a
   disposable brush, apply a thin layer
   of glue to the surface and gently lay
   the napkin into the glue. Carefully
   apply a thin layer of glue over top
   of napkin.
4. Repeat the gluing process to cover box
   lid and mask with napkins. Let dry.
5. Paint bottom of box with black
   acrylic paint. Let dry.
6. Dry brush gold acrylic paint over
   box to antique it. Let dry. Place
   decoupaged lid on box.
7. Paint bamboo stick with black
   acrylic paint. Let dry. Hot glue to
   left side of mask.
8. Thread beads on tie at top of tassel.
   Hot glue tie to inside of mask. ❏

## SUPPLIES

**Glues:**

Decoupage glue

All purpose, super strength adhesive gel

**Surface:**

Wooden waste bin, painted color of
your choice

**Papers for Decoupage:**

Scrapbook papers, 4 sheets in coordinating prints

**Embellishments & Trims:**

Glass mosaic tiles, 1/4" or 1/2"

4 wooden balls, 3/4" diameter, painted
color of your choice

**Other Supplies:**

Waxed paper

**Tools:**

Pencil

Scissors

Disposable brush

Straight pin

# It's a Mod, Mod World Waste Bin

Scrapbook papers are absolutely great for decoupage, and this
mod print is very cool when you accent it with glass tiles in
a mosaic pattern around the top of the box. Fill the box with
magazines or a leafy plant, or use it as a trendy wastebasket.

## INSTRUCTIONS

1. With a pencil, trace around one side
   of box onto one piece of scrapbook
   paper. Cut out.
2. With a disposable brush, apply a thin
   coat of decoupage glue on one side
   of box.
3. Working quickly while glue on box is
   wet, lay scrapbook paper face down
   on waxed paper. Brush decoupage
   glue over entire back of paper. Place
   paper face up on wet glue on box.
   Smooth out bubbles or wrinkles with
   your fingers. Prick any remaining

bubbles with a pin and press flat
with your fingers.
4. Apply a coat of decoupage glue over
   the paper, sealing the edges.
5. Repeat gluing process to cover all
   four sides of box.
6. Work on one side of box at a time.
   Arrange glass tiles in a pleasing
   design. Glue to top rim of box with
   super strength adhesive gel. Let dry
   overnight.
7. Hot glue ball feet to bottom of box
   with super strength glue. ❑

## SUPPLIES

**Glues:**

Decoupage glue

Hot glue gun & glue sticks

**Surface:**

Wooden birdhouse of your choice *(unpainted)*

**Papers for Decoupage:**

Assorted tissue papers with romantic designs of your choice

**Embellishments & Trims:**

Assorted buttons

Yarn and fibers of your choice

**Other Supplies:**

"Amore" rubber stamp

Permanent black ink pad

*Optional:* Spray sealer, clear

**Tools:**

Scissors

Disposable foam brush

Metal edge ruler

18kt gold paint pen

Pompom tool – or cut your own from cardboard

### PattieWack Pointer:

This birdhouse is for decorative use indoors. If you want to use it outdoors as a functional birdhouse, omit the pompom, and spray with three protective layers of clear sealer, letting it dry thoroughly.

# Romantic Rendezvous Birdhouse

Lovebirds will enjoy this little birdhouse as a decorative accent, for exchanging notes, or as a delightful reminder that love is in the house!

## INSTRUCTIONS

1. Cut tissue to fit panels of sides and roof of birdhouse.
2. Work on one panel at a time. With a foam brush, apply a thin coat of decoupage glue and glue the tissue to the birdhouse. Brush a layer of glue on top of tissue, sealing the edges.
3. Repeat the gluing process to cover all sides and roof of birdhouse. Let dry.
4. Accent edges of birdhouse with gold paint pen. Run pen tip down edges in a straight line, using a ruler if necessary.
5. Stamp the word "Amore" in several places in a random pattern.
6. Hot glue a row of overlapping buttons around bottom edge of roof.
7. Make a 2" pompom, using coordinating yarn & fibers. *(See "How to Make a Pompom" in the "Live a Little Pompom Pillow" project, Chapter 2.)*
8. Hot glue pompom to top point of birdhouse roof. ❏

# A Moment in Time Camera Case

Capture a moment in time when you decoupage copies of cherished family photos to an antique camera case. Colorize the photos with pale pastel paints for an extra helping of nostalgia.

## SUPPLIES

**Glue:**
Decoupage glue

**Surface:**
Antique leather camera case *(or leather purse, journal, box, etc.)*

**Papers for Decoupage:**
Color copies of old photos *(do not use original photos)*

**Paint:**
Acrylic paint, pale pastel colors of your choice

**Other Supplies:**
Waxed paper

**Tools:**
Scissors
Foam brush
Cotton swabs for tinting photos

## INSTRUCTIONS

1. Cut out color copies of photos.
2. Apply a very light touch of pastel paint with a cotton swab to accent a dress or other items that you want to stand out in the photos. Let dry.
3. Lay photos on case for placement. Mark with pencil if needed.
4. With a foam brush, apply a thin layer of decoupage glue on the place for first photo.
5. Lay first photo face down on waxed paper. Brush a layer of glue on back. Place photo face up onto wet decoupage glue on case. Press out any air bubbles with your fingers.
6. Apply a thin coat of glue over photo, sealing the edges.
7. Repeat the gluing process with remaining photos. Let dry. ❑

# Express Yourself
# Lapboard & Clipboard

When I thumb through magazines, I'm always on the hunt for images I would love to use in my decoupage projects. This is a great way to get children involved in art, as they express themselves with decoupage on a clipboard or artist's lapboard.

## SUPPLIES

**Glue:**
Decoupage glue, matte

**Surface:**
14" x 18" artist's lapboard, or regular clipboard

**Papers for Decoupage:**
Magazine clippings

**Embellishments & Trims:**
Alphabet stickers
Scraps of ribbon and trims

**Paint:**
Ultra flat black spray paint

**Other Supplies:**
Paper towels
Clear spray varnish, satin

**Tools:**
Scissors
Soft-bristle brush
Straight pin
*Optional:* Brayer

## INSTRUCTIONS

1. In a well-ventilated area, preferably out-doors, spray both sides of clipboard or lapboard with flat black paint. Let dry. Spray a second coat. Let dry.
2. Cut out images from magazines that are interesting to you, or to the recipient, if it is going to be a gift.
3. Brush a thin layer of decoupage glue on back of cutout image, being careful to cover completely to the edges. Place on clipboard, and press with fingers or brayer to flatten bubbles. Prick bubbles with a pin, if necessary. Wipe off any excess glue with a damp paper towel.
4. Repeat until you have glued all cutout images on front and back of clipboard. Let dry thoroughly.
5. Spray front and back of clipboard with two coats of clear varnish. Dry thoroughly after each coat. ❏

# No Rules
# Window Mannequin Collage

Imagine my excitement when I found this papier mache mannequin at a flea market for two dollars! I knew immediately that it was perfect for a decoupage collage. I made the miniature dollhouse window the focal point of the piece as a window to the artistic soul. You could use this collage technique on a chair, a table, a lampshade, or any flat surface. Remember, when you are creating a collage, "the rules have flown out the window."

## SUPPLIES

**Glues:**
Decoupage glue
All purpose, super strength adhesive gel
*Optional:* hot glue gun & glue sticks

**Surface:**
Mannequin *(or table, chair, lampshade, etc.)*

**Papers for Decoupage:**
Magazine clippings, scrapbook papers, gift wrap, etc.

**Embellishments & Trims:**
Clear cabochons, gems, and crystals
*Optional:* 3-dimensional objects of your choice *(dollhouse window, for example)*

**Paint:**
Black spray paint

**Other Supplies:**
Waxed paper
Spray sealer, clear

**Tools:**
Scissors
Soft acrylic brush

## INSTRUCTIONS

1. In a well-ventilated area, preferably outdoors, spray base piece with black paint. Let dry 24 hours.
2. Cut out images from magazines.
3. Apply a thin coat of decoupage glue to base piece in an area large enough for a selected cutout.
4. Working quickly while glue is wet, lay cutout face down on waxed paper. Brush decoupage glue over entire back of cutout. Place cutout face up on wet glue on surface. Smooth out any bubbles with your fingers.
5. Apply a coat of decoupage glue over cutout, sealing the edges.
6. Continue gluing cutouts over entire piece as you desire. Let dry.
7. Protect the completed collaged piece with spray sealer. The sealer is especially important on chairs or tables.
8. Adhere gems and crystals with adhesive gel.
9. Attach 3-dimensional objects with hot glue, if desired. ❑

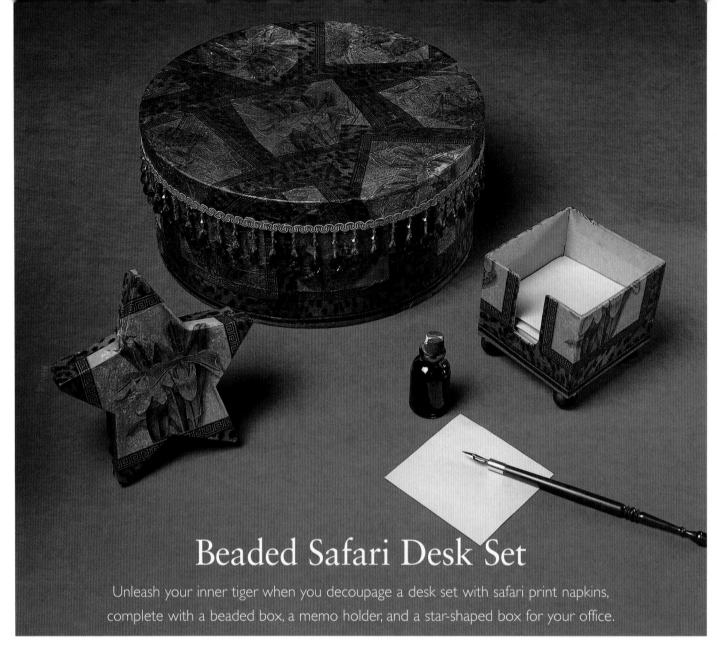

# Beaded Safari Desk Set

Unleash your inner tiger when you decoupage a desk set with safari print napkins, complete with a beaded box, a memo holder, and a star-shaped box for your office.

## SUPPLIES

**Glues:**
Decoupage glue
Hot glue & glue sticks

**Surfaces:**
Round papier mache box
Papier mache memo holder
Star-shaped papier mache box

**Papers for Decoupage:**
Paper napkins with tiger or leopard theme
Paper napkins with coordinating colors and designs

**Embellishments & Trims:**
Beaded fringe

**Other Supplies:**
4 wooden balls, 1/2", painted to match memo holder

**Tools:**
Scissors
Disposable brush

## INSTRUCTIONS

1. Separate napkin plies. Discard all but the printed top ply.
2. Arrange napkins on surfaces to determine best placement.
3. Apply one napkin at a time. With a disposable brush, apply a thin layer of glue to the surface and gently lay the napkin into the glue. Carefully apply a thin layer of glue over top of napkin.
4. Repeat the gluing process to cover surfaces with napkins. Let dry.
5. Glue wooden ball feet to bottom of memo holder.
6. Hot glue beaded fringe to round box. ❏

# CHAPTER 11

# Just for Kids

The key words for kids' glues are "non-toxic" and "easy cleanup!" Doing crafts with enthusiastic small children is noisy, messy fun. As they grow older, you will enjoy introducing kids to increasingly complex projects and more challenging materials.

## Glues to Use

Kid's craft glue
Foam glue
Fabric glue
Glue stick
White craft glue

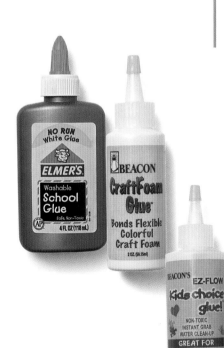

# SUPPLIES

**Glue:**

Kid's craft glue

**Surfaces:**

Tall bottles (wine bottles are a good shape)

2 foam balls, 3" diameter

**Embellishments & Trims:**

Chenille stems

Plastic gems, eyelashes, bell, chain, ribbon, etc.

**Paint:**

Black spray paint

Black tempera paint

**Other Supplies:**

Felt squares-1 each black, pink, brown, camouflage

**Tools:**

Craft sticks

Brush for tempera paint

Blunt end scissors

Rubber bands

# Fifi & Fido Bottle Pets

These perfectly poised pets have plenty of character. When you prepare the bottles and foam balls in advance, even small children can make them with glue, felt, and basic craft supplies.

Patterns

# INSTRUCTIONS

1. Prepare bottles ahead of time. In a well-ventilated area, preferably outdoors, spray bottles with black paint. Let dry.
2. Prepare foam balls ahead of time. Spear foam balls with craft sticks, and paint with black tempera paint. Place sticks in bottles to hold while drying.
3. Cut out felt shapes for the kids to create their own characters, or use the patterns to cut out parts for cat and dog.
4. Glue foam balls to tops of bottles.
5. Glue front legs and back legs to bases of bottles. Hold in place with rubber bands while drying.
6. Glue faces and ears to foam balls. Poke chenille stems into the balls for whiskers.
7. Glue chenille stems to backs of bottles for tails.
8. Glue on felt neckties, gems, and eyelashes.
9. Attach chains, bells, and ribbon. ❏

# On a Roll Containers

Kids love crafting these containers for pencils, pens, or "whatever."
Their retro look also works in a teenager's room or a college dorm.

## SUPPLIES

**Glues:**
Glue stick
White craft glue

**Surface:**
Container to be covered (ice cream
    tub, coffee can, etc.)

**Embellishments & Trims:**
Plastic clothesline

**Other Supplies:**
Magazines

**Tools:**
Scissors
Pencil

## INSTRUCTIONS

*Young children can use white craft glue
instead of hot glue, and hold the rolls in
place with rubber bands until the glue sets.*

1. Cut out colorful magazine pages that
   have no text printed on the page.
2. Roll pages from corner to corner, around
   a pencil. Glue paper with a glue stick as
   you roll. Pull out pencil. Repeat rolling
   pages until you have enough to cover
   sides of container.
3. Glue rolled pages to sides of container,
   letting rolls protrude past top and
   bottom of container. Trim off excess
   length with scissors for a neat edge.
4. Cut plastic clothesline into 3" lengths.
   Push one end of the first piece of plastic
   clothesline into top opening of one of the
   rolls. Skip next roll, and push the other
   end into the second roll from the first.
5. Push a second piece of plastic clothesline
   into opening of skipped roll, and push
   the other end into the second roll from
   the first.
6. Push a third piece of plastic clothesline
   into the same roll as the end of the first
   piece of plastic clothesline, and push the
   other end into the second roll from the
   first. Continue around top and bottom
   of container to finish edges. ❑

Fig. 1

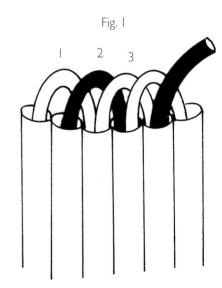

# Silly Spoons Puppets

Kids' imaginations will bring these goofy characters to life.
Don't be surprised if the spoons develop voices and
personalities as children put buttons, felt, and basic craft
supplies together to give their spoons faces and costumes.

## PattieWack Pointers:

Print out the faces from family photos. Cut them out and glue to the
spoon to create some really silly puppets for your family to play with!
You can make a great puppet stage by placing a spring tension rod
across a doorway or a closet door. Hang a brightly colored curtain
that just touches the floor; children can trip over a curtain that is too
long. Now you have an instant theater!

## SUPPLIES

**Glues:**
Kids' craft glue

**Surface:**
Wooden spoon

**Embellishments & Trims:**
Buttons for eyes or nose
Yarn or feather boa for hair

**Other Supplies:**
8" x 20" cotton fabric
Rubber band
Felt in assorted colors

**Tools:**
Scissors

## INSTRUCTIONS

1. Tear fabric into an approximate size of 8" x 20".
2. Gather fabric around base of spoon to create a collar and skirt. Hold fabric onto spoon handle with a rubber band.
3. Cut a strip of felt to cover the rubber band. Wrap around rubber band and glue into place.
4. Cut felt triangles, squares, circles, and eyelashes to create facial features.
5. Glue felt eyes and mouth to spoon. Glue a button for the nose.
6. Glue loops of yarn to back of spoon for hair. Other ideas for hair: a snippet of a feather boa, strips of felt, or loops of ribbon. ❑

## SUPPLIES

**Glues:**
Permanent spray adhesive
Fabric glue

**Surface:**
Umbrella

**Embellishments & Trims:**
Pompoms, purchased or handmade from
   yarn and fibers of your choice *(See "How
   to Make a Pompom" in the "Live a Little
   Pompom Pillow" project, Chapter 2.)*
Glitter
Google eyes
Glitter pens

**Other Supplies:**
Felt squares, colors of your choice
Newspaper

**Tools:**
Scissors

# Monster Umbrellas Party Decor

These crazy cool umbrellas are great for Mommy
or Daddy to carry on a trick-or-treat outing
with the kids. Hang several from the ceiling for
party decorations. Or have a crafting party for
the whole family by cutting out different shapes
and letting the kids create their own scary or
fun faces to glue onto their Monster Umbrellas!
These monsters won't hold up in the rain —
they're for fun and decoration only.

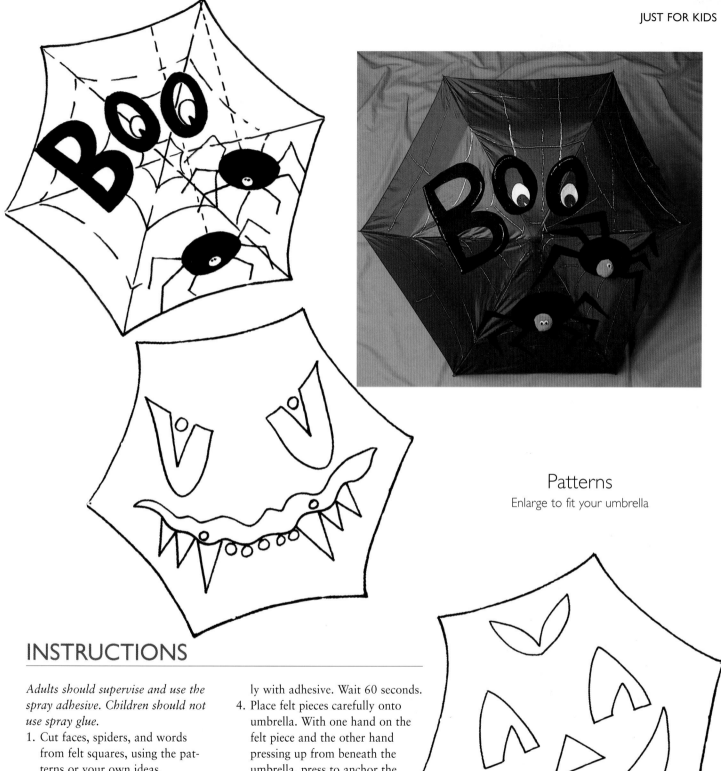

## Patterns
Enlarge to fit your umbrella

# INSTRUCTIONS

*Adults should supervise and use the spray adhesive. Children should not use spray glue.*

1. Cut faces, spiders, and words from felt squares, using the patterns or your own ideas.
2. If you would like to cover felt pieces with glitter, lay them face up on newspaper. Spray with adhesive and immediately sprinkle glitter over the piece. Let dry.
3. Turn felt pieces face down on newspaper. Spray backs complete-

ly with adhesive. Wait 60 seconds.
4. Place felt pieces carefully onto umbrella. With one hand on the felt piece and the other hand pressing up from beneath the umbrella, press to anchor the adhesive.
5. Adhere google eyes and pompoms with fabric glue, holding in place until the glue has set.
6. Draw spider web and other embellishments with glitter pens. ❏

# CHAPTER 12

# Glue Recipes

Years ago, if you wanted to stick things together, your mom would grab a few ingredients out of the kitchen cabinet and stir up a nice little bowl of glue for you. Today's moms can mix up some of these tried and true recipes for tons of fun for their kids on a rainy afternoon. Store your glue potions in airtight containers with proper labels and keep in a cool dry place.

## Basic Glue

3 Tablespoons cornstarch
4 Tablespoons cold water
2 cups boiling water
Squeeze-type container

Mix cornstarch and cold water in a small bowl. Pour into the boiling water, stirring constantly. When liquid is clear and thick, remove from heat and let cool. Pour into a plastic squeeze container and label.

## Basic Paste

3/4 cup cold water
1/2 cup flour
3 cups boiling water
Squeeze-type container

Slowly pour cold water into flour as you stir to make a paste. Pour paste into the boiling water, stirring constantly. Cook for 5 minutes or until the paste is thick and smooth. When cool, pour into a plastic squeeze-top container and label. This paste is great for papier mache projects. It will last for months if you keep it in the refrigerator.

## Sticker Glue

2 parts white craft glue
1 part vinegar

Combine two parts white craft glue with one part vinegar and mix thoroughly. Apply to surfaces with a paintbrush and allow to dry for 6-10 seconds. Activate the glue by applying water to it. Keep in an airtight container.

## Library Paste

1 cup flour
1 cup sugar
1 teaspoon alum
4 cups water
30 drops oil of cloves

Mix all ingredients in a saucepan and cook until clear and thick. Add oil of cloves and mix well. Store in a covered container.

## Puffy Paste

1 part shaving cream
1 part white craft glue
*Optional:* Food coloring

Mix equal parts shaving cream and glue. Add food coloring for color if you want. Use a craft stick to stir and to put paste on paper. The mixture will puff up when it dries.

## Slime

1 cup water
1 Tablespoon borax *(available in laundry supplies section of supermarket)*
1/4 cup water
1/4 cup white glue
*Optional:* Food coloring
Plastic bag with zip seal

Stir borax into 1 cup water until completely dissolved (approximately 4% solution). Combine 1/4 cup water with white glue, mixing thoroughly. In the plastic bag, add equal parts borax solution and glue solution; 1/2 cup of each will make a cup of slime. Add a couple of drops of food coloring if desired. Seal bag and knead the mixture. Store your slime in the sealed bag or an airtight container in the refrigerator to keep it longer.

## Funny Putty

2 parts white craft glue
1 part liquid starch

Gradually pour starch into glue as you mix. If mixture is sticky, add more starch. Cover and refrigerate overnight. This funny putty can be cut with scissors and can be pulled or twisted.

# Faux Porcelain Roses
# Bread Dough Jewelry

Knead white bread and glue together with a drop of paint. That's all you need to create this simple clay. The delicate roses in the jewelry set will inspire you to try all kinds of shapes with this easy recipe.

## SUPPLIES

**Glue:**
White tacky glue

**Surface:**
Bread dough clay

**Embellishments & Trims:**
Decorative paper clips in spiral, flower, and heart shapes
Jewelry findings – jump rings, clasps, etc.

**Tools:**
Needle nose pliers

### Bread Dough Clay Recipe:

1 slice white bread
1 Tablespoon white tacky glue
Acrylic paint (for colored clay)
Plastic bags
Craft stick

1. Remove crust from bread and discard crust. Tear bread into small pieces. Put into a disposable cup or bowl.
2. Add 1 tablespoon of tacky glue. Mix with craft stick until well blended.
3. Divide into thirds to make three different colors. Add a few drops of acrylic paint to each batch. Mix with craft stick, then knead in your hands until it becomes the consistency of fine clay. Keep bread dough in plastic bags to keep it from drying out while you make the roses.

Photo 1

Photo 2

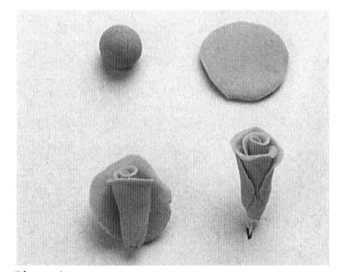
Photo 3

## INSTRUCTIONS

1. Take a pinch of dough and roll it into a ball. Flatten ball into a circle. Roll circle into a cylinder to form center of rose. (See Photo 1.)
2. Take another pinch of dough and roll it into a ball. Flatten ball into a circle. Shape circle into a petal. Press petal to center of rose. (See Photo 2.)
3. Continue to make petals and add to the rose until it is the size you desire. (See Photos 3 & 4.)
4. Pinch any excess clay from bottom of rose. Roll excess clay into a ball and flatten it into a circle. Press a spiral paper clip into clay circle. Place clay rose over paper clip and press it gently into the clay circle to encase the clip. Set aside to dry.
5. Repeat the process until you have enough roses on clips to form a bracelet or necklace. Let dry overnight.
6. Join rose clips together with jump rings and add clasps to complete jewelry. ❑

### PattieWack Pointers:

Clay objects made with this recipe can be glued to all sorts of projects, such as frames, buttons, journals, boxes, and scrapbook pages. Adhere them to any hard surface with white tacky glue, adhesive dots, or hot glue.

Photo 4

# Mosaic Madness
# Grout Recipe

If you've got glue and sand, you've got grout! This crafter's grout recipe is not meant for outdoors, but it is great for indoor mosaic projects. The best part is that you don't have to wait for the mosaic pieces to dry. The project is done all at one time.

### Grout Recipe

Sand (beach sand or craft sand)
White tacky glue
Acrylic paint (for colored grout)
Disposable spatula and bowl

Mix sand and glue in a disposable bowl until the consistency is very thick like grout, but still spreadable. Add a few drops of acrylic paint for colored grout.

## SUPPLIES

**Glues:**
Grout

**Surface:**
Wooden stool

**Embellishments & Trims:**
Alphabet brads
Buttons

**Paint:**
Spray paint, color of your choice

**Other Supplies:**
Broken china or tiles
*Optional:* Buttons, cup handles, marbles, etc.
Large plastic bag
Towel
Spray sealer, clear

**Tools:**
Hammer

## INSTRUCTIONS

1. In a well-ventilated area, preferably outdoors, spray wooden stool with paint. Let dry completely.
2. Place china or tiles inside plastic bag, lay on towel, and break with hammer into small pieces, no larger than 2" across.
3. Apply 1/4" thickness of grout to top of stool, in a small area approximately 6" x 6".
4. Push broken china into grout, pushing down with your fingers until grout comes up around edges of china. Add pieces 1/4" apart, until you have covered all of the grout.
5. Apply more grout in another 6" x 6" area. Add more china pieces. Include interesting pieces of broken tiles, old buttons, or even a coffee cup handle.
6. Spell words with metal alphabet brads by bending the prongs over so they can be pushed into the grout.
7. Continue to cover top of stool with grout and mosaics.
8. Let dry and cure for 7 days.
9. Spray with sealer. *(Note: This project is for indoor use only.)* ❑